LEVEL TWO ▼ MIXED

ESSENTIAL REPERTOIRE

FOR THE DEVELOPING CHOIR

BY
JANICE KILLIAN
MICHAEL O'HERN
LINDA RANN
EDITED BY
EMILY CROCKER

ISBN 978-0-7935-4339-7

HAL•LEONARD®
CORPORATION
7777 W. BLUEMOUND RD. P.O. BOX 13819 MILWAUKEE, WI 53213

AUTHORS

Dr. Janice Killian, Music Education
Texas Woman's University, Denton, Texas

Michael O'Hern, Choral Director
Lake Highlands Junior High
Richardson Independent School District, Texas

Linda Rann, Choral Director
Dan F. Long Middle School
Carrollton-Farmers Branch Independent School
District, Texas

PROJECT EDITOR
Emily Crocker
Director of Choral Publications
Hal Leonard Corporation, Milwaukee, Wisconsin

PRODUCTION EDITOR
Ryan French
Choral Editor
Hal Leonard Corporation, Milwaukee, Wisconsin

CONSULTANTS
Glenda Casey, Choral Director
Berkner High School
Richardson Independent School District, Texas

Bobbie Douglass, Choral Director
L. D. Bell High School
Hurst-Euless-Bedford Independent School District,
Texas

Jan Juneau, Choral Director
Klein High School
Klein Independent School District, Texas

Dr. John Leavitt, Composer and Conductor
Wichita, Kansas

Brad White, Choral Director
Richland High School
Birdville Independent School District, Texas

Printed in the United States of America

Send all inquiries to:
Hal Leonard Corporation
7777 W. Bluemound Rd., Box 13819
Milwaukee, WI 53213

CONTENTS

1 **BARBARA ALLEN**   English Folk Song
arranged by Linda Spevacek

9 **CHI LA GAGLIARDA**   Baldassare Donato
edited by Maynard Klein

16 **DADME ALBRICIAS, HÍJOS D'EVA**   Sixteenth Century Villancico
edited by Noah Greenberg

22 **THE FALCON**   Mary Lynn Badarak

30 **GATHER YE ROSEBUDS**   Andrea Klouse

41 **GLORIA**   Franz Joseph Haydn
edited by John Leavitt

48 **GLORIA IN EXCELSIS**   Antonio Vivaldi
edited by William Herrmann

58 **HOME ON THAT ROCK**   Kirby Shaw

65 **I WILL SING THE GOODNESS OF THE LORD**   Emily Crocker

77 **IN PRIDE OF MAY**   Thomas Weelkes
arranged by Steven Porter

83 **JE LE VOUS DIRAI!**   Pierre Certon
edited by John Leavitt

90 **JUBILANCE**   Linda Spevacek

102 **JUBILATE DEO**   Emily Crocker

114 **MASTERS IN THIS HALL**   Traditional Carol
arranged by Catherine Bennett

122 **NEVER TELL THY LOVE**   Houston Bright

126 **O BELLA FUSA**   Orlando di Lasso
edited by Maynard Klein

133 **O OCCHI MANZA MIA**   Orlando di Lasso
edited by Maynard Klein

138 **SIX FOLK SONGS**   Johannes Brahms
   139   **I'D ENTER YOUR GARDEN**
   142   **THE FIDDLER**
   146   **HOW SAD FLOW THE STREAMS**
   149   **AT NIGHT**
   153   **AWAKE, AWAKE**
   157   **A HOUSE STANDS 'NEATH THE WILLOW'S SHADE**

CONTENTS (cont.)

162 THE SKY CAN STILL REMEMBER   Michael A. Gray

168 SONG FOR A RUSSIAN CHILD   Andrea Klouse

179 THREE SPANISH CAROLS   Traditional Spanish Carols
                                                   arranged by Emily Crocker

  180   PASTORES Á BELÉN
  186   ¿QUE REGALO?
  192   ADORAR AL NIÑO

200 TUTTO LO DI MI DICI "CANTA"   Orlando di Lasso
                                                   edited by Maynard Klein

208 WHEN I WAS ONE AND TWENTY   Robert Rhein

215 WITH A VOICE OF SINGING   Martin Shaw

226 GLOSSARY

 **TO THE STUDENT**

Welcome to choir!

The reason students join choir are as diverse as the students themselves. Whatever your reason may be, this book was designed to help you achieve your particular goal. The many different types of songs in this book have been selected to fit your voice and allow you to be successful. In music, just as in many other activities, practice, effort, and dedication will pay off. Your study of choral music can develop skills that you will enjoy throughout your entire life. Best wishes for your musical success!

Student Expectations Checklist:

- Take responsibility for your own development as a musician.
- Every time you sing, make it a quality experience.
- Work to master the basic musical skills.
- Develop an attitude of wanting to improve every day.
- Be willing to try new things.
- Display an attitude of effort at all times.
- Come to class prepared to work and learn.
- Be present for all rehearsals and performances.
- Listen carefully during rehearsals. Critical listening improves the quality of a choir.
- Show a willingness to work with others.
- Choir is a "group" effort, but every individual counts. Working together is the key.
- Respect the effort of others.
- Practice concert etiquette at all times, especially during rehearsals.
- Make a positive contribution, don't be a distraction to the choir.
- Enjoy experiencing and making beautiful music.

BARBARA ALLEN
Composer: Folk Song, arranged by Linda Spevacek
Text: English Folk Song
Voicing: SATB

Cultural Context:
This ballad, "Barbara Allen," is among the most popular of all English-Scottish folk songs brought to America. (A *ballad* generally tells legendary tales of past events.) It has been said that over two hundred versions of this song exist; some have been published, but most remain part of our folk tradition. Linda Spevacek has taken this familiar melody and created a choral arrangement full of lush harmony and a feeling of sadness. The story tells of William, who dies of a broken heart because his true love, Barbara Allen, does not love him in return. Upon finding out about William's death, Barbara Allen is consumed with guilt and dies the next day. In its original form, the poem goes on to finish the story:

> Sweet William was carried to one churchyard, Miss Barbara to another.
> A briar grew out of one of their graves, a rose tree out of the other.
> They grew as high as the old church top, they could not grow any higher
> They bound and tied in a true love's knot, for all true lovers to admire.

Musical Terms:

rit. (ritardando)	*mf* (mezzo forte)	*a tempo*
f (forte)	*div.* (divisi)	*mp* (mezzo piano)
stagger breathing	*rit. poco* (poco ritardando)	𝄐 (fermata)
ballad		

Preparation:
There are many unison sections in "Barbara Allen." They help create the mood of the piece. Perfect unisons can be very difficult to sing.

Try to sing the following short phrase from Barbara Allen. Begin with just a few voices and add voices one at a time, carefully listening to sound like "one voice." Be sure to keep the vowel sounds tall in the word "adieu." (adieu = ah-dyoo).

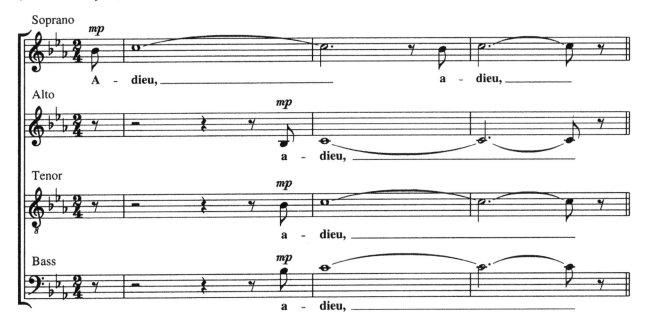

Evaluation:
Tell the story of Barbara Allen and William in your own words. What events do you think led up to William's death? Be creative!

Barbara Allen

For SATB and Piano

Harmonization and Choral Arrangement
by LINDA SPEVACEK

English Folk Song

dwell-in', ____ Made ev'ry youth cry__ "Well-a-day," her name was Bar- b'ra

dwell-in', ____ Made ev'ry youth cry__ "Well-a-day," her name was Bar- b'ra

Al- len. _____

Al- len. _____

mf
'Twas in the

mf
'Twas in the

mf
'Twas in the

mf
'Twas in the

merry month of May, and all the green buds were

merry, merry, merry month of May, and all the green buds were

merry, merry, merry month of May, and all the green buds were

merry month of May, and all the green buds were

swellin', _____ Young William there on his death-bed lay _____ for

swellin', _____ Young William there on his death-bed lay _____ for

swellin', _____ Young William there on his death-bed lay _____ for

swellin', _____ Young William there on his death-bed lay _____ for

5

bet-ter can I___ ev-er___ be if I can't have Bar-b'ra Al- len.___

bet-ter can I___ ev- er___ be if I can't have Bar-b'ra Al- len.___

He turned his

He turned his

pale face ____ in- to the wall, ____ for in him death was

pale face ____ in- to the wall, ____ for in him death was

dwell-in'. ____

dwell-in', ____

A- dieu, a- dieu my __ friends all a- round, be kind to Bar- b'ra

A- dieu, a- dieu my __ friends all a- round, be kind to Bar- b'ra

CHI LA GAGLIARDA (COME DANCE THE GALLIARD)

Composer: Baldassare Donato (ca. 1525-1603), edited by Maynard Klein
Text: Italian, English text by Maynard Klein
Voicing: SATB a cappella

Cultural Context:

Baldassare Donato produced a collection of villanellas in 1550. "Chi la Gagliarda" probably came from that collection. Villanellas were light-hearted madrigal-like pieces originating in Naples, Italy. They often were written to make fun of more sophisticated and serious madrigals of the time. This particular villanella includes a galliard, a quick triple-time dance popular in the 16th century Italy. The galliard had complicated dance steps which included exaggerated leaps.

Musical Terms:

(Note: Renaissance music generally did not have dynamic, tempo, or style markings. These have been added by the editor.)

allegro esuberante

mp (mezzo piano)

mf (mezzo forte)

(crescendo and decrescendo)

⌢
℗ (fermata)

¢ (cut time)

‖: :‖ (repeat signs)

molto ritmico e giocoso

rit. (ritardando)

polyphonic

villanella

galliard

Preparation:

Rehearse the Italian by reading the following:

Italian:
Pronunciation:

Chi la Gagliarda, donne, vo'imparare,
kee lah gahl-LYAHR̃-dah DOHN-neh voh(ee)m-pah-R̃AH-r̃eh

Venite a noi che siamo mastri fini,
veh-NEE-teh ah NOH(ee) keh s(ee)AH-moh MAH-str̃ee FEE-nee

Che di se-ra e di mattina mai manchiamo di sonare.
keh dee seh-R̃AH eh dee mah-TEE-nah MAH-ee mahn-kee-AH-moh dee soh-NAH-r̃eh

Tan ti ra.
tahn tee r̃ah

* r̃ = rolled or flipped r

Evaluation:

After you have learned "Chi la Gagliarda," listen to each section sing their part and evaluate the Italian pronunciation. Then trade tasks until each section has sung and been evaluated.

Since "Chi la Gagliarda" begins *polyphonically* (different parts enter at different times so that different words are sung at the same time) it is especially important to evaluate each section separately. If you are precise with your pronunciation within a section, the entire piece will combine more effectively.

Chi la Gagliarda
(Come Dance The Galliard)

For SATB a cappella

English Text by MAYNARD KLEIN

By BALDASSARE DONATO (ca. 1525-1603)
Edited by MAYNARD KLEIN

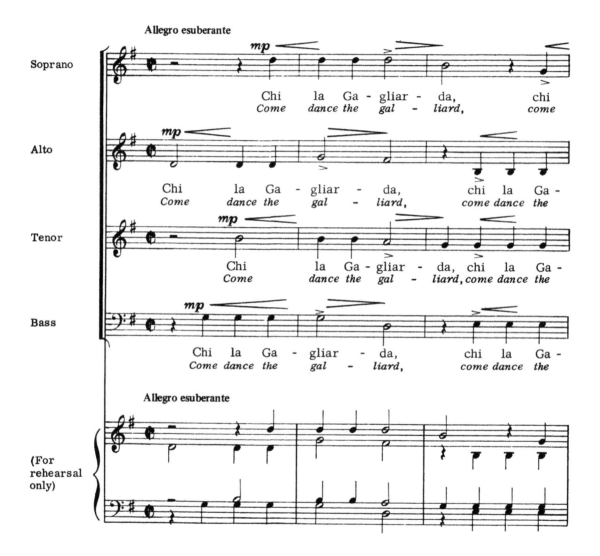

-stri fi - ni, ma-stri fi - ni, ma - stri fi -
-ter danc - ers, mas - ter danc - ers, mas - ter danc -

-stri fi - ni, ma-stri fi - ni, ma - stri fi -
-ter danc - ers, mas - ter danc - ers, mas - ter danc -

-stri fi - ni, ma-stri fi - ni, ma - stri fi -
-ter danc - ers, mas - ter danc - ers, mas - ter danc -

-stri fi - ni, ma-stri fi - ni, ma - stri fi -
-ter danc - ers, mas - ter danc - ers, mas - ter danc -

ni, Che di se - rae di mat - ti - na, mai man-chia -
ers, From the ev'n-ing un - til morn - ing, we are danc -

ni, Che di se - rae di mat - ti - na, mai man-
ers, From the ev'n - ing un - til morn - ing, we are

ni, Che di se - rae di mat - ti - na mai man-
ers, From the ev'n - ing un - til morn - ing, we are

ni, Che di se - rae di mat - ti - na mai man-
ers, From the ev'n - ing un - til morn - ing, we are

mo, mai man - chia - mo di so - na - re.
ing, we are danc - ing, we are danc - ing.

chia - mo, mai___ man-chia-mo di so - na - re.
danc - ing, we___ are danc-ing, we are danc - ing.

chia - mo, mai___ man-chia-mo di so - na - re.
danc - ing, we___ are danc-ing, we are danc - ing

chia - mo, mai___ man-chia-mo di so - na - re.
danc - ing, we___ are danc-ing, we are danc - ing.

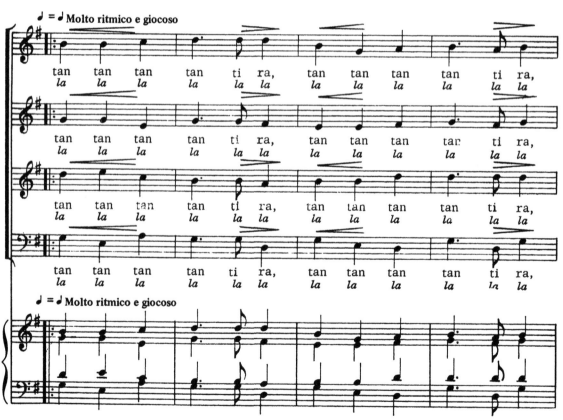

♩ = ♩ Molto ritmico e giocoso

tan tan tan tan ti ra, tan tan tan tan ti ra,
la la la la la la la la la la la la

tan tan tan tan ti ra, tan tan tan tan ti ra,
la la la la la la la la la la la la

tan tan tan tan ti ra, tan tan tan tan ti ra,
la la la la la la la la la la la la

tan tan tan tan ti ra, tan tan tan tan ti ra,
la la la la la la la la la la la la

♩ = ♩ Molto ritmico e giocoso

tan tan ti - ra, tan tan tan tan ti ra tan tan ti
la la la la la la la la la la la la la

tan tan ti - ra, tan tan tan tan ti ra tan tan ti
la la la la la la la la la la la la la

tan tan ti - ra, tan tan tan tan ti ra tan tan ti
la la la la la la la la la la la la la

tan tan ti - ra, tan tan tan tan ti ra tan tan ti
la la la la la la la la la la la la la

rit.

ra, tan tan tan tan ti - ra, tan tan ti - ra.
la la la la la la la la la la la.

ra, tan tan tan tan ti - ra, tan tan ti - ra.
la la la la la la la la la la la.

ra, tan tan tan tan ti - ra, tan tan ti - ra.
la la la la la la la la la la la.

ra, tan tan tan tan ti - ra, tan tan ti - ra.
la la la la la la la la la la la.

rit.

DADME ALBRICIAS, HÍJOS D'EVA (SONS OF EVE, REWARD MY TIDINGS)

Composer: Sixteenth Century Villancico, edited by Noah Greenberg
Text: From "Villancicons de diuersos Autores..." (1556), English text by Hubert Creekmore
Voicing: SATB a cappella

Cultural Context:

Catalan, a Spanish dialect spoken in the northeast corner of Spain, is the language of the text of this Spanish carol. "Dadme albricias, híjos d'Eva" is an example of the *villancico*, a type of vocal music from Spain written during the *Renaissance Period* (1450-1600). These songs were *a cappella* (voices only) with *homophonic* sections (all voices with same rhythm and words starting together) contrasting with *polyphonic* sections.

Characteristics of polyphonic music:

- Each voice part is independent (has a different melody).
- Each voice part enters at a different time, rarely do all parts enter together.
- Each voice part imitates the other (parts are similar, but usually not identical).
- Voice parts are seldom singing the same words at the same time.

Musical Terms:

Solo	Tutti	Solo ad lib.
⌢ $\widehat{\rho}^{\bullet}$ (fermata)	polyphonic	homophonic
villancico	Renaissance	

Preparation:

- As you study this piece, identify which sections are written in homophonic style and which are written in polyphonic style. Write in your music the letter H above the start of homophonic sections and write the letter P above the start of polyphonic sections. (The solo sections are already marked.)

- To prepare for the staggered entrances of the voice parts, practice the following exercise by tapping, chanting, or conducting each part individually, then together.

Evaluation:

After you have learned to perform this song well, listen to a taped performance of your choir. Based on what you hear, respond to the following statements:

- I was able to identify the homophonic and polyphonic sections.
- I was able to hear a difference between the two sections.
- The staggered entrances were sung correctly and clearly heard.

Dadme albricias, híjos d'Eva

(Sons of Eve, Reward My Tidings)

For SATB a cappella

English Text by
HUBERT CREEKMORE

Sixteenth Century Villancico
Edited by NOAH GREENBERG

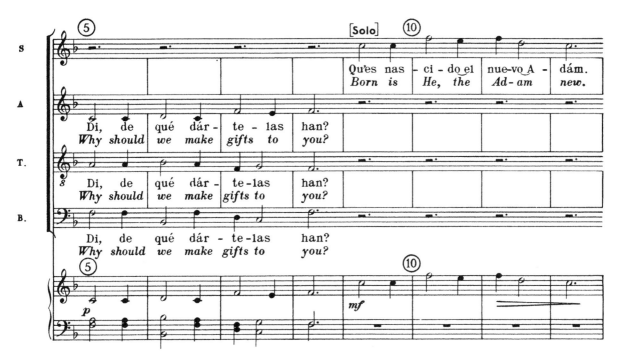

19

20

THE FALCON
Composer: Mary Lynn Badarak
Text: Anonymous
Voicing: SAB

Cultural Context:
As you read the text of this poem, notice the sadness expressed by the young maiden over the death of her lover. The falcon that carried her knight away may represent death itself.

Lully Lullay, the falcon hath bourne my love away.
He bare him up, He bare him down, He bare him into an orchard brown.
Lully Lullay, the falcon hath bourne my love away.

There was a great hall hang'd with purple and pall,
There was a bed and that bed was red and gold.
Lully Lullay, the falcon hath bourne my love away.

And in that bed there lay a knight, his wounds bleeding day and night,
And by that bedside knelt a maiden weeping day and night.
Lully Lullay, the falcon hath bourne my love away.
(Pray, let him stay, bourne him away, lullay.)

Musical Terms:

dolce	***p*** (piano)	***mf*** (mezzo forte)
———————— (crescendo)	———————— (decrescendo)	più mosso
allarg. ed dim. (allargando ed diminuendo)		*rit.* (ritardando)
a tempo	𝄐 (fermata)	più lento

Preparation:
Practice speaking and singing tall vowels found in words in this song.

lullay	loo-leh (not loo-lay)
love	lahv (not luhv)
up	ahp (not uhp)
away	ah-weh(ee)
down	dah(oo)n
brown	brah(oo)n
my	mah(ee)
night	nah(ee)t

Evaluation:
Create your own story to establish the scenario of this poem. Where is it taking place? What is the time period? Who are the two love characters? How does your story end? Share your story with other members of the class. Visualize your story as you perform this song.

The Falcon

For SAB and Piano

Text is Anonymous

Music by MARY LYNN BADARAK

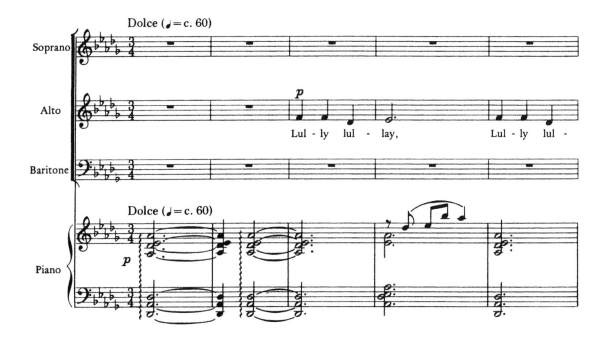

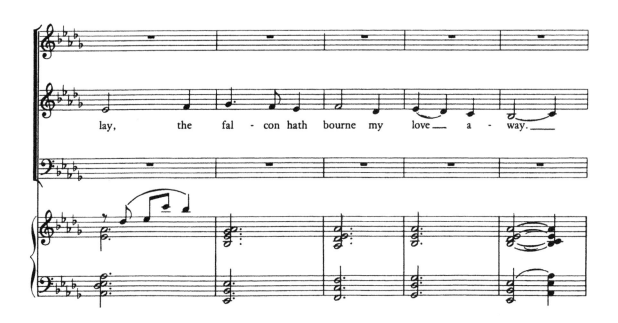

He bare him up _____ He bare him down, _____ He bare him

in - to an or-chard brown. Lul - ly, _____ Lul - ly lul - lay, _____

Lul - ly lul - lay, Lul - ly lul -

Lul - ly lul - lay, the fal - con hath bourne ____ my love a - way.

lay, ____ the fal - con hath bourne my love ____ a - way. _____

24

25

26

27

And by that bed-side knelt a maid-en, weep-

And in that bed there

ing, weep - ing, weep -,ing day and night, _

There knelt a maid weep-ing, weep - ing day and

was_ a knight bleed - ing ___ day and night,

Lul - ly,_ lul - lay, weep - ing, day and night,_ Lul - ly ___ lu - ly lul -

night, _ Lu - ly lul - lay,

Lul - ly, lul - lay, Lu - ly lul - lay,

GATHER YE ROSEBUDS
Composer: Andrea Klouse
Text: Robert Herrick (1591-1674) [adapted]
Voicing: SATB

Cultural Context:
Andrea Klouse, a contemporary composer who lives and writes in Tacoma, Washington, is known for her beautiful melodies and sensitive musical settings. The text for "Gather Ye Rosebuds" was written by the poet Robert Herrick around 1648. Poets have often made analogies between flowers and human feelings and situations. For example, compare the meaning of "Gather Ye Rosebuds" with the text of Brahms' "I'd Enter Your Garden" on p. 140 in this book.

Musical Terms:

freely and legato	(♩ = 76)	Unis. (unison)
mp (mezzo piano)	*cresc.* (crescendo)	*mf* (mezzo forte)
decresc. (decrescendo)	*f* (forte)	*div.* (divisi)
poco cresc. (poco crescendo)	*pp* (pianissimo)	*p* (piano)
a tempo	*rit.* (ritardando)	*molto rit.* (molto ritardando)
sfp (sfzorzando piano)	morendo	rubato

Preparation:
Always read texts carefully before you sing. The better you understand a text the more effective you will be when you convey those ideas to your audience. Answer the questions below, as you read and think about the meaning of the text to "Gather Ye Rosebuds."

> *Gather ye rosebuds while ye may, Old Time is still a-flyin'.*
> *And this same flower that smiles today tomorrow will be a-dyin'.*
>
> *Glorious lamps of heaven's sun, still higher, higher are gettin',*
> *And sooner will their race be won, the nearer he is to settin'!*
>
> *The age is best which is the first so while ye may go marry;*
> *For having lost but once your prime you may forever tarry,*
>
> *Lully, lullulay, lullulay, while you may forever tarry.*
>
> *Gather ye rosebuds while ye may. Old Time is still a-flyin',*
> *For this fine flower, this fine flower, tomorrow will be a-dyin'.*

Consider: Who or what is "Old Time"?
What "race" is the poet speaking of in verse two?
Why might the lullaby sounds be put in the poem? What might they mean?
Think of examples in which it is best to "gather ye rosebuds while ye may."

Evaluation:
This text was written in 1648. Do you think this text applies today? Why or why not?

Commissioned by the Seattle Girls' Choir for their Gala Tenth Anniversary Celebration Concert,
March 29, 1992, Dr. Jerome Wright, Conductor

Gather Ye Rosebuds

For SATB and Piano

Text by ROBERT HERRICK (1591-1674) [adapted]　　　　　　　　Music by ANDREA KLOUSE

while   ye   may,   Old   Time   is

still _____ a — fly — in'.   And __

this   same   flow — er   that   smiles   to —

mar - ry; _____ For hav - ing

lost   but   once   your   prime   you

may   for - ev - er   tar -

* Pronounced "loo-lee, loo—loo-lay"
** Measures 68 through 74 may be performed a cappella

40

GLORIA (from *Heiligmesse*)
Composer: Franz Joseph Haydn (1732-1809), edited by John Leavitt
Text: Latin from Liturgical "Gloria" of The Mass
Voicing: SATB

Cultural Context:

Franz Joseph Haydn, born in Austria, is regarded as one of the most influential composers of the eighteenth century. Although he is best known for his instrumental writing (symphonies and string quartets), he also wrote vocal music in the form of operas, masses, and oratorios. The *Heiligmesse* (Holy Mass), written for four soloists, chorus, and full orchestra, is one of six festival masses Haydn wrote late in his life.

Musical Terms:

vivace	f (forte)	p (piano)
Unis. (unison)	‖: :‖ (repeat signs)	

Preparation:

As you prepare to learn this well-known work, practice correct Latin diction and word stress. Be careful not to "punch" or over-stress the ends of words or phrases.

Latin: *Gloria in excelsis Deo.*
Pronunciation: GLAW-r̃ee-ah een ehk-SHEHL-sees DEH-aw

                Et in terra pax hominibus.
                eht een TEH-r̃ah pahks aw-MEE-nee-boos

                Bonae voluntatis
                BAW-neh vaw-loon-TAH-tees

                Laudamus te, benedicimus te
                lah(oo)-DAH-moos teh beh-neh-DEE-chee-moos teh

                Glorificamus te.
                GLAW-r̃ee-fee-KAH-moos teh

                                        * r̃ = rolled or flipped r

Translation: "Glory to God in the highest and on earth peace to all of good will. We praise thee. We bless Thee. We adore Thee. We glorify Thee."

Evaluation:

As you sing this piece, check yourself on the following:
- Are you singing DEH-aw (not deh-AW)?
- Are you singing vaw-loon-TAH-tees (not vaw-loon-tah-TEES)?
- Are you singing GLAW-r̃ee-fee-KAH-moos teh (not glaw-r̃ee-fee-kah-moos TEH)?

Singing with correct word stress may take a lot of practice. You can do it!

Gloria

(From HEILIGMESSE)

For SATB and Piano

Edited by JOHN LEAVITT

By FRANZ JOSEPH HAYDN (1732-1809)

44

vo - lun - ta - tis.

Lau - da - mus te, be - ne - di - ci - mus

te, a - do - ra - mus

Unis.

45

GLORIA IN EXCELSIS (from *Gloria*)
Composer: Antonio Vivaldi (ca. 1678-1741), edited by William Herrmann
Text: Latin from the Ordinary of the Mass, English text by William Herrmann
Voicing: SATB

Cultural Context:

Antonio Vivaldi taught and composed in a girls' orphanage in Venice when he wrote *Gloria*. In *Gloria*, Vivaldi takes each phrase of the Gloria (the second of the five parts of the Catholic mass) and devotes an entire movement to it. "Gloria in Excelsis" is the opening movement.

Vivaldi lived during the *Baroque Period* of music history. Characteristics of the Baroque include:

- terraced dynamics - suddenly loud, suddenly soft, very little gradual dynamic change. Notice the piano and forte dynamic markings in your music.

- constantly moving accompaniment. Notice the repeated eighth notes in the piano accompaniment.

Musical Terms:

allegro	*f* (forte)	*p* (piano)
⌢ (fermata)	Baroque	terraced dynamics

Preparation:

Prepare for singing the Latin text by speaking the following:

Latin: *Gloria in excelsis Deo*
Pronunciation: GLAW-ree-ah een ehk-SHEHL-sees DEH-aw

As you sing the ♩. ♪ pattern, be sure to articulate the sixteenth note by singing a "flipped" R. To practice this, sing a D instead of an R.

GLAW - dee - ah   *etc.*

Evaluation:

After you have learned the rhythms and pitches in "Gloria in Excelsis," tape record your choir singing the piece. Pay special attention to how you are pronouncing the Latin.

Are you singing tall vowels throughout?
- Is "glo" of "gloria" pronounced "glaw" rather than "gloh"?
- Is "in" pronounced "een" rather than the American "in"?
- Is "De" of "Deo" pronounced "deh" rather than "day"?

Gloria in excelsis

(from GLORIA)

For SATB and Piano

English Text by
WILLIAM HERRMANN

By ANTONIO VIVALDI (ca. 1678-1741)
Edited and keyboard reduction
by WILLIAM HERRMANN

50

(a) As though written $\mathbf{c}$ $\textit{♩}$ $\textit{♩}$ | $\textit{♩}$ $\textit{♩}$ | $\textit{♩}$ $\textit{♩}$ | (b) Slightly accent notes marked — and <u>avoid</u> accenting
in ex-cel-sis De-o   those marked ⌣.

51

52

glo - ri - a, glo - ri - a in ex -
glo - ri-ous, glo - ri-ous God in

glo - ri - a, glo - ri - a in ex -
glo - ri-ous, glo - ri-ous God in

glo - ri - a, glo - ri - a in ex -
glo - ri-ous, glo - ri-ous God in

glo - ri - a, glo - ri - a in ex -
glo - ri-ous, glo - ri-ous God in

cel -
high -

cel -
high -

cel -
high -

cel -
high -

(a) Simpler alternate version: m.51 etc.

54

(a) Simpler alternate version: m. 53

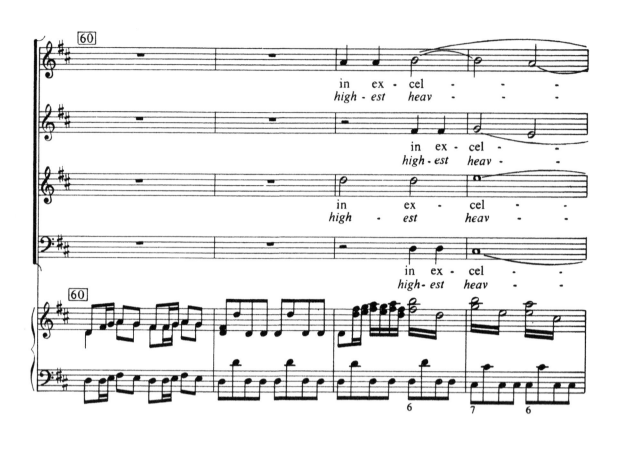

in ex - cel -
high - est heav -

in ex - cel -
high - est heav -

in ex - cel -
high - est heav -

in ex - cel -
high - est heav

6   7   6

- sis,
- en,

- sis,
- en,

- sis,
- en,

- sis,
- en,

7   6   7

glo-ri-a   in ex-cel-sis De - o.
Glo-ri-ous in the high-est heav - en.

glo-ri-a   in ex-cel-sis De - o.
Glo-ri-ous in the high-est heav - en.

glo-ri-a   in ex-cel-sis De - o.
Glo-ri-ous in the high-est heav - en.

glo-ri-a   in ex-cel-sis De - o.
Glo-ri-ous in the high-est heav - en.

HOME ON THAT ROCK
Composer: Kirby Shaw
Text: Kirby Shaw
Voicing: SAB a cappella

Cultural Context:
"Home On That Rock" was written for the Albert McNeil Jubilee Singers (a famous African American professional choral group from California) and is an energetic *a cappella* selection with a gospel flavor. The use of interesting rhythms, clapping, and stomping add to the style of the piece.

Kirby Shaw is a composer and arranger specializing in vocal jazz who lives in Oregon.

Musical Terms:

swing	simile	> ♪ (accent)
p (piano)	*pp* (pianissimo)	*mf* (mezzo forte)
f (forte)	*mp* (mezzo piano)	——————— (crescendo)

Preparation:
A great deal of rhythmic precision is necessary when performing the syncopated rhythms of "Home on that Rock." Syncopation is a rhythmic pattern that stresses notes on the "off beat." Try to be rhythmically precise when practicing this song. Chant the following rhythmic pattern:

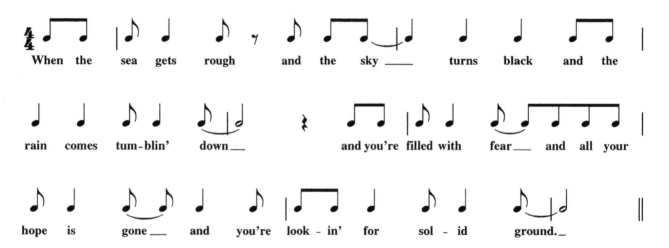

Evaluation:
After learning the pitches and rhythms at letter A, do the following:
- In sections, sing your part, making sure that the syncopated rhythms are clear and precise.
- Listen for rhythmic clarity as well as correct pitches.

Find and practice other examples of syncopation in this piece.

Home on that Rock

For SAB a cappella

Words and Music by
KIRBY SHAW

*small notes optional, sing SSAB meas. 9-14, 36-41, 68-73.

** ♩ = *ascending smear – slide into note from 2-3 steps below. Reach pitch*
just prior to next note or rest. Slight accent.

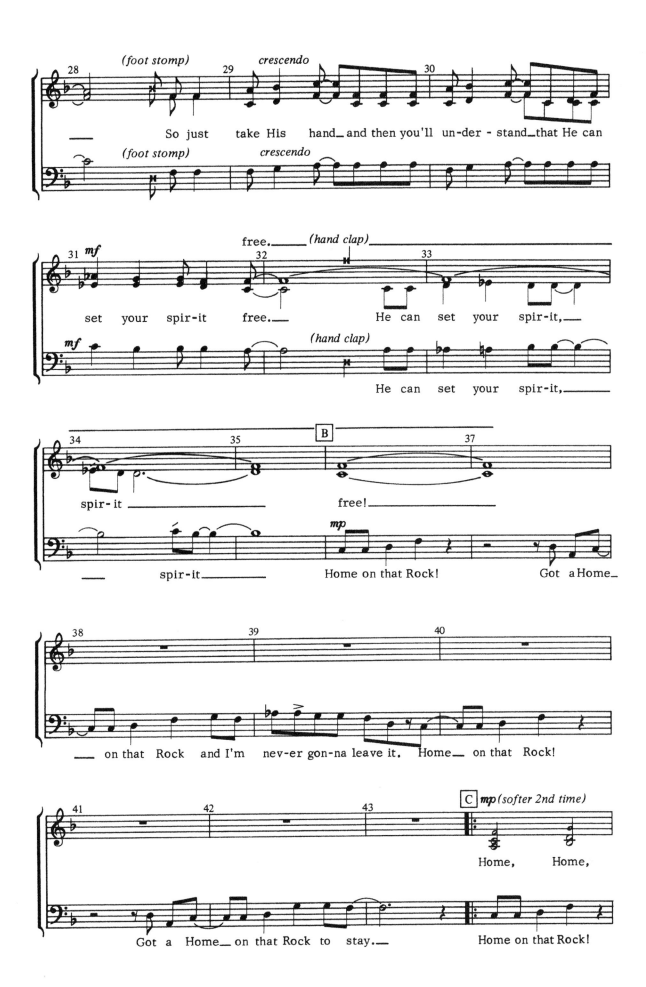

62

63

I WILL SING THE GOODNESS OF THE LORD

Composer: Emily Crocker
Text: Psalm 89, adapted
Voicing: SATB with Optional Descant

Cultural Context:

"I Will Sing the Goodness of the Lord" is an uplifting piece to learn and to perform. The 6/8 meter gives it drive to the end. Emily Crocker was commissioned to write this piece in 1988 for an honor choir in Houston, Texas.

Musical Terms:

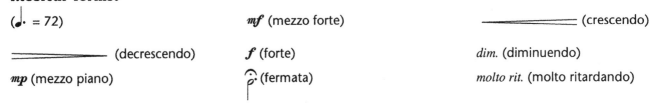

(♩. = 72)   *mf* (mezzo forte)   ———————— (crescendo)

———————— (decrescendo)   *f* (forte)   *dim.* (diminuendo)

mp (mezzo piano)   𝄐 (fermata)   *molto rit.* (molto ritardando)

Preparation:

There are a few spots in this song where the rhythm needs extra attention. In measure 15 the Sopranos, Tenors, and Basses have the same rhythm and words, while the Altos sing something different. Practice saying the words in rhythm.

Measure 15:

Measure 33 also features a challenging rhythm pattern for Sopranos and Altos.

Measure 33:

Evaluation:

Listen to an audio recording of your choir's performance and evaluate your progress. Identify the areas in which the choir did very well, and the areas that need improvement, based on the following:

- Focus your attention on measures 15 and 33. Were the rhythms sung correctly?

- Were there other sections of the song which could have been performed better? List the specific measures. Identify the problem.

- Continue to practice until you are pleased with the quality of performance.

For the 1988 T.M.E.A. Region IX Junior High Choir
Brad White, Conductor

I Will Sing the Goodness of the Lord

For SATB with optional Descant and Piano

Psalm 89

Music by EMILY CROCKER

for - ev - er, for - ev - er.

I will sing__ the good - ness of__ the Lord.__

I will pro-claim your truth.

Through all a - ges I will pro - claim your truth.

Through all a - ges I will pro-claim your truth.__

I am sure__ your love__ will last for - ev - er,

I am sure your love will last for - ev - er,

and your truth shall en - dure   as___ the heav - ens.___

heav   -   ens.

and your truth shall en - dure   as   the   heav - ens.

I will sing___ the good - ness of___ the   Lord.

Sop. **mp** 33

The heav-ens shall praise Thy won - ders.___

Ten. **mp**

The

69

For - ev - er

For - ev - er,

I will sing____ the good - ness of____ the Lord.____

more.

for - ev - er.   Blest are they____ that know the joy - ful

Blest are they   that know   the joy - ful

The joy - ful sound, the joy - ful sound._____

sound._____ They shall walk in the

sound._____ They shall walk in the

The light of Thy coun - te - nance,

coun - te - nance,_____

light of_____ Thy coun - te - nance,

light of Thy coun - te - nance,_____

and re - joice in____ Thy name.____

and re - joice all the day in____ Thy name.____

and re - joice all the day in Thy name.____

In Thy good - ness, they shall be lift - ed

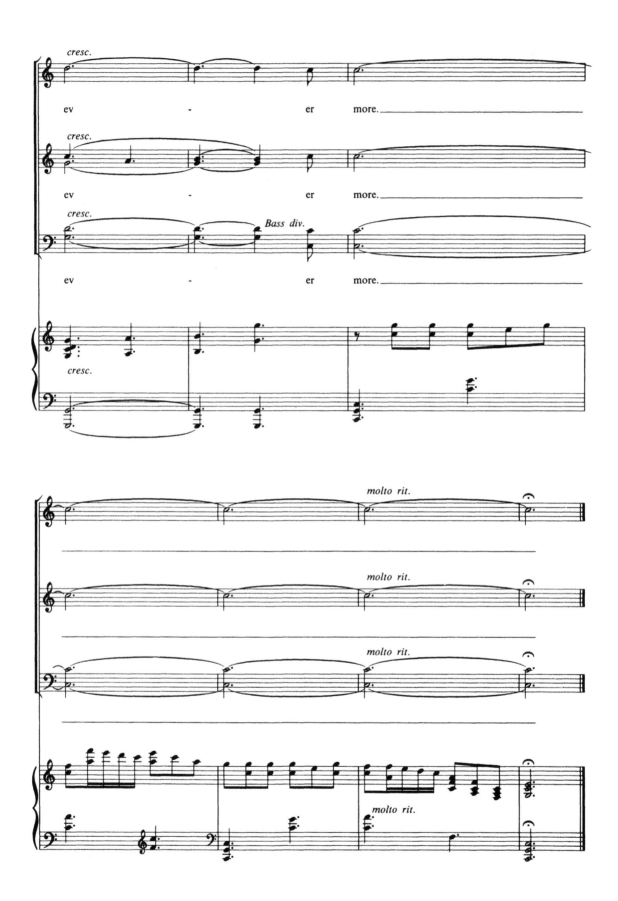

ev - er more._____

ev - er more._____

Bass div.

ev - er more._____

cresc.

molto rit.

molto rit.

molto rit.

molto rit.

IN PRIDE OF MAY

Composer: Thomas Weelkes (1575-1623), arranged by Steven Porter
Text: Thomas Weelkes
Voicing: (S)SATB a cappella

Cultural Context:

Thomas Weelkes, an English composer, lived during the *Renaissance* when madrigals were very popular. A *madrigal* is a vocal *a cappella polyphonic* song written in four to six parts. The voice parts sometimes enter at different times. The text in English madrigals can often be described as *pastoral,* or about nature. Can you imagine the birds singing on the "fa-la-la" sections of "In Pride of May"?

Musical Terms:

($\quad$ = 72)	*rit.* (ritardando)	————————— (decrescendo)
p (piano)	(fermata)	*mf* (mezzo forte)
(accent)	*a tempo*	*pp* (pianissimo)

Preparation:

Notice the staggered entrances of Soprano 1, 2, and Alto at the beginning of this piece. (Tenors and Basses enter at different times two measures later.)

- Speak the words in rhythm.
- Sing the pitches on a "zah" syllable.
- Sing with text. Remember to keep your mouth in the "ah" shape (tall inside) when you sing "in."

Examples:

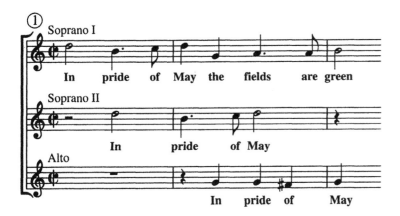

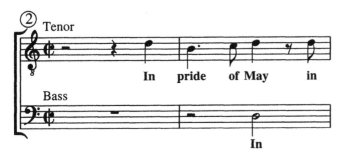

Evaluation:

As you evaluate an audio or video performance of your choir performing this piece, respond to the following questions:

- Are the staggered entrances precise and clearly understood?
- Is there dynamic contrast between the *forte* and *piano* echo sections?
- Does the energy level remain strong in the *piano* sections?
- Does the choir maintain a light, dance-like style throughout the piece?

These checks will help you and your choir sing in an authentic Renaissance style.

In Pride of May

For (S)SATB a cappella

Arranged by
STEVEN PORTER

Words and Music by
THOMAS WEELKES (1575-1623)

81

JE LE VOUS DIRAI! (DO NOT DARE I SAY IT)
Composer: Pierre Certon (ca. 1510-1572), edited by John Leavitt
Text: French, English translation by John Leavitt
Voicing: SATB a cappella

Cultural Context:

French composer, Pierre Certon, was a choirmaster in Paris for most of his life. His writings consisted primarily of *masses*, *motets*, and *chansons*.

"Je le vous dirai!" is an excellent example of a *Renaissance* French chanson. In French, the word chanson has two meanings, one being the word for "song," and the other referring to a specific type of song. During Certon's lifetime in the 16th century, the chanson was a very popular style with over 1500 versions printed in Paris alone. At that time these songs were light, fast, *a cappella* pieces in four parts (SATB) commonly featuring text about love. They were all written in French.

In this song, the storyteller debates whether he should share his gossip or not. He knows of a jealous man and his wife who live in the village, but does not want to speak ill of them. Finally, the storyteller decides to "say it anyway!"

Musical Terms:

(♩ = 60)	*mf* (mezzo forte)	*p* (piano)
﹐ (breath mark)	*poco rit.* (poco ritardando)	*a tempo*
pp (pianissimo)		

Preparation:

To learn this song more quickly and easily, it is helpful to look at the form or organization of the song. This song is in **ABABA** form. Many sections are repeated which makes it easier to learn. Label your music as follows:

Section A:	The "la, la, la" section (mm. 1-7)
Section B:	The first verse "Il est un homme..." (mm. 8-15)
Section A:	Repeat of "la, la, la" section (mm. 16-22)
Section B:	The second verse "Il n'est pas..." (mm. 23-30)
Section A:	Repeat of "la, la, la" section (mm. 31-end)

Evaluation:

As you perform "Je le vous dirai!," listen carefully and identify the form of the piece.

- Can you hear a contrast between the different sections?
- Can you tell when one section ends and the other begins?
- Do the repeated sections make the song easier for you to learn?

Je le vous dirai!

(Do not dare I say it)

For SATB a cappella

<table>
<tr><td>English Translation by
JOHN LEAVITT</td><td>By PIERRE CERTON (ca.1510-1572)
Edited by JOHN LEAVITT</td></tr>
</table>

85

Je le vous di - rai, et La, la, la, **Je** le vous di - rai!
I will tell you now, and La, la, la, I will tell you now.

Je le vous di - rai, et La, la, la, **Je** le vous di - rai!
I will tell you now, and La, la, la, I will tell you now.

Je le vous di - rai, et La, la, la, **Je** le vous di - rai!
I will tell you now, and La, la, la, I will tell you now.

Je le vous di - rai, et La, la, la, **Je** le vous di - rai!
I will tell you now, and La, la, la, I will tell you now.

89

JUBILANCE
Composer: Linda Spevacek
Text: Linda Spevacek
Voicing: SATB

Cultural Context:
"Jubilance" was written in 1990 for the Westwood Junior High Chorale in Richardson, Texas. Linda Spevacek lives and works in Tempe, Arizona. The original text is written in the style of a psalm text.

"Jubilance" is full of contrasts. The contrasting sections and dynamics indicated in the music add greatly to the excitement of this piece. Can you can identify the seven contrasting sections found in "Jubilance"?

Musical Terms:

ff (fortissimo)   *div.* (divisi)   *p* (piano)

f (forte)   *mf* (mezzo forte)   **Tempo I**

molto rit. (molto ritardando)   *8va* (octave above)   ———————— (crescendo)

molto cresc. e accel. (molto crescendo and accelerando)   *loco*

Preparation:
"Jubilance" is full of long phrases that must be sung on one breath. Sing the following phrase from "Jubilance" in unison on one breath. Carry the breath all the way through the cut-off.

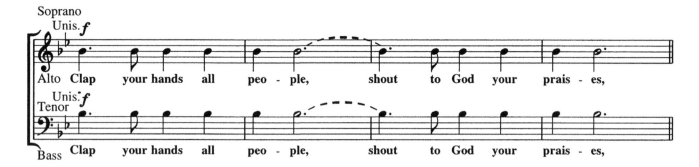

Evaluation:
Find the phrase "God the artist, God the painter..." at mm. 41-48.
- Sing each of these on one breath.
- Sing them again with the dynamics indicated in the music. Good singers perform more than the notes on the page. They sing expressive phrases.

Commissioned for the 1991 Texas Music Educators Association Convention
by the Westwood Junior High School Chorale, Lindy Perez, Director

Jubilance

For SATB and Piano

Words and Music by LINDA SPEVACEK

let your heart be joy - ful with sing - ing! _____ Al - le -

let your heart be joy - ful with sing - ing! _____ Al - le -

let your heart be joy - ful with sing - ing! _____ Al - le -

let your heart be joy - ful with sing - ing! _____ Al - le -

lu - ia! _____ Sing your praise to

lu - ia! _____ Sing your praise to

lu - ia! _____ Sing your praise to

lu - ia! _____ Sing your praise to

* Divisi preferred if possible

God!

God!

God!

God!

94

95

O be joy - ful now in har - mo - ny.

O be joy - ful now in har - mo - ny.

O be joy - ful now in har - mo - ny.

O be joy - ful now in har - mo - ny.

Clap your hands all peo - ple, shout to God your prais - es,

Clap your hands all peo - ple, shout to God your prais - es,

Clap your hands all peo - ple, shout to God your prais - es,

Clap your hands all peo - ple, shout to God your prais - es,

let your heart be joy - ful with sing - ing!_____ Al - le -

let your heart be joy - ful with sing - ing!_____ Al - le -

let your heart be joy - ful with sing - ing!_____ Al - le -

let your heart be joy - ful with sing - ing!_____ Al - le -

lu - ia!_____ Sing your praise to

lu - ia!_____ Sing your praise to

lu - ia!_____ Sing your praise to

lu - ia!_____ Sing your praise to

100

JUBILATE DEO
Composer: Emily Crocker
Text: Psalm 100
Voicing: SATB

Cultural Context:
Emily Crocker wrote "Jubilate Deo" for the 1986 Georgia All-State Junior High Mixed Chorus. It has since become a favorite among choirs across the nation.

"Jubilate Deo" is written in contrasting styles. The first part is energetic, fast, and accented. Label it "A." The second section (beginning at measure 29) is marked *dolce* (sweetly) and is to be sung in a soft, sustained manner. Label it "B." Are there any any sections of this piece which repeat?

Emily Crocker lives in Milwaukee, Wisconsin, and has written over one hundred compositions.

Musical Terms:

f (forte)

poco a poco cresc. (poco a poco crescendo)

——————— (crescendo)

espressivo

div. (divisi)

mp (mezzo piano)

marcato

ff (fortissimo)

dolce

——————— (decrescendo)

p (piano)

$\frown$ (fermata)
o

poco rit. (poco ritardando)

più

Preparation:
"Jubilate Deo" can be very exciting to perform, but it has certain challenges. One challenge is to sing the descending half steps in tune.

- Sing the following descending half step intervals. Remember that a half step is the smallest interval that you sing.
- To practice singing descending half steps in tune, point upward and gradually move your hand up as you sing.

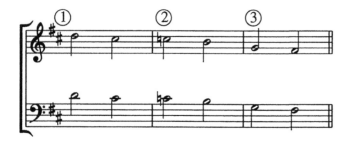

Evaluation:
- Find the half step intervals in your music. Circle these spots in your music.
- Which set of letters best describes the structure of "Jubilate Deo"? A B or A B A?

For the 1986 Georgia All-State Junior High Mixed Chorus,
Joyce Eilers Bacak, Director

Jubilate Deo

For SATB and Piano

Psalm 100

Music by EMILY CROCKER

106

113

MASTERS IN THIS HALL
Composer: Traditional Carol, arranged by Catherine Bennett
Text: William Morris (1834-1896)
Voicing: 3-Part Mixed Voices with Optional Descant

Cultural Context:
This familiar carol comes to us from England by way of France. Edmund Sedding, the English compiler of Christmas carols, was given this old French melody by the organist of Chartres Cathedral in France. Sedding then asked a co-worker, William Morris, to write an English text to fit the tune. Morris, a well-known poet, painter, and inventor (he designed the comfortable, cushioned Morris chair) tried to capture the medieval flavor of the ancient French tune. Sedding published the melody with Morris' words as "Masters in This Hall" in his *Ancient Christmas Carols* in 1860.

Catherine Bennett, a choral composer who lives in Olympia, Washington, has arranged each section of "Masters in this Hall" differently. One time it is sung by Basses only; one time it is a round; and one time it is unison choir with descant. Such variety makes an exciting setting of this familiar carol.

Musical Terms:

(♩. = 116)	*mf* (mezzo forte)	‖: :‖ (repeat signs)
𝄋 (segno)	———————— (crescendo)	⊕ Coda
mp (mezzo piano)	**D.S. al Coda**	unison
f (forte)	descant	(first ending, second ending)
cresc. (crescendo)	*ff* (fortissimo)	⸓ (staccato)

Preparation:
At first glance, this piece may be confusing because of all the repeats and other markings. Prepare by doing the following:

1. Find the following symbols in your music: ⊕ 𝄋
2. Look up the meanings of any you do not know in your glossary.

Use the Evaluation section below to check how well you understand and can apply these symbols.

Evaluation:
Place the correct measure number in the blank beside the words. You will need to know what to do when you see repeats (‖: :‖), 1st and 2nd endings, dal segno (𝄋), coda (⊕). When you are finished you will have a listing of the order in which each line should be sung.

Measure #   Words
_____   *Masters in this hall,*
_____   *Noel, noel, noel! Noel sing we clear!*
_____   *Noel, noel, noel! Noel sing we loud!*
_____   *This is Christ, the Lord,*
_____   *Noel, noel, noel! Noel sing we clear!*
_____   *Noel, noel, noel! Noel sing we loud!*
_____   *Masters in this hall,*
_____   *Noel, noel, noel! Noel sing we clear!*
_____   *Noel, noel, noel! Noel sing we loud!*
_____   *Cast down the proud!*

Masters in this Hall

For 3-Part Mixed and Piano with Optional Descant

Words by
WILLIAM MORRIS (1834-1896)

Traditional Carol
Arranged by CATHERINE BENNETT

brought from o - ver sea; pray, hear ye what I say.

13 % *Both endings on D.S.*

No - el, no - el, no - el! No - el sing we
No - el, no - el, no - el! No - el sing we

No - el, no - el, no - el! No - el sing we
No - el, no - el, no - el! No - el sing we

13 % *Both endings on D.S.*

clear! Hol - pen* are all folk on earth,____ born the
loud! God to - day hath poor men rais - ed up, and

clear! Hol - pen* are all folk on earth,____ born the
loud! God to - day hath poor men rais - ed up, and

*"Holpen" - Old English for "helped" or "aided"

118

119

NEVER TELL THY LOVE

Composer: Houston Bright (1916-1970)
Text: William Blake (1757-1827)
Voicing: SATB a cappella

Cultural Context:

Houston Bright was a professor and composer-in-residence at West Texas State University in Canyon, Texas.

William Blake was an English poet who lived from 1757-1827. Some of his most famous works are the *Songs of Innocence* and *Songs of Experience*. In addition to being a renowned poet, Blake was also a talented artist and illustrator.

"Never Tell Thy Love" speaks of life, love, and death with great expression and symbolism. The traveler mentioned in the poem has been said to symbolize death.

Musical Terms:

meno mosso	*pp* (pianissimo)	*a tempo*
mf (mezzo forte)	——————— (crescendo)	// (caesura)
poco più mosso	——————— (decrescendo)	*p* (piano)

Preparation:

Word stress is very important to "Never Tell Thy Love."

Say the following text in rhythm stressing where indicated. The stressed syllables are written in capital letters.

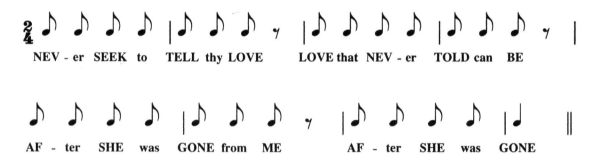

Evaluation:

To check your understanding of stressed and unstressed syllables, find the words printed above in your music (mm. 1-4).

- Sopranos, Altos, and Tenors sing together, emphasizing the word stress.
- Add the Bass "pedal tone" part, and sing it together.
- As you sing, do you hear a difference between the stressed and unstressed syllables?

For the Texas Interscholastic League Music Festivals
F.W. Savage, State Director

Never Tell Thy Love

For SATB a cappella

Text by
WILLIAM BLAKE (1757-1827)

Music by
HOUSTON BRIGHT (1916-1970)

123

124

after she was gone, A trav-el-ler came by _____ in-

after she was gone, A_ trav-el-ler came by _____ Si-lent-ly, in-

after she was gone, A trav-el-ler came by _____ Si-lent-ly, in-

gone from me, A_ trav-el-ler came by _____ Si-lent-ly, in-

vis-i-bly: He took her with a sigh. _____

vis-i-bly: He took her with a sigh. _____

vis-i-bly: He took her with a sigh. _____

vis-i-bly: He took her with a sigh.

125

O BELLA FUSA (THE SPINNING WHEEL)
Composer: Orlando di Lasso (1532-1594), edited by Maynard Klein
Text: Orlando di Lasso, English text by Maynard Klein
Voicing: SATB a cappella

Cultural Context:

Orlando di Lasso lived from 1532 to 1594 near the end of the *Renaissance.* He was born in Belgium, but lived in Italy for ten years and spent the last thirty-four years of his life in Germany. Di Lasso was a notable figure in sixteenth century choral music as both a singer and composer. He composed over two thousand compositions during his lifetime. For more information about di Lasso, see "O occhi manza mia" on p. 135.

"O bella fusa" is an example of a lighter form of Italian vocal writing called a *canzonetta* meaning "little song." Canzonetti were written for *a cappella* singing (voices only) with evenly phrased sections which were usually repeated. The Italian text usually was not of a serious nature. Most interesting was the use of text and melody to create images or feeling. For example, if a song referred to heaven, the voice part would move upward. Di Lasso used this technique to create the sound of a spinning wheel in "O bella fusa."

Musical Terms:

(Note: Renaissance music did not include dynamic, tempo, or style markings. Any markings found in this score have been supplied by the editor.)

moderato grazioso	*mf* (mezzo forte)	━━━━━━ (crescendo)
━━━━━━ (decrescendo)	*p* (piano)	*mp* (mezzo piano)
f (forte)	*cresc.* (crescendo)	⌢ₒ (fermata)
canzonetta		

Preparation:

In a canzonetta phrases are often repeated. Search the music for the answers to these questions.

- As you look at the music and words of "O bella fusa" can you find sections which are repeated?
- How many repeated sections can you find in this song?
- Are you asked to sing the repeated section with the same or different dynamic level?

Evaluation:

If sung correctly, as you sing "O bella fusa" in Italian, your choir should sound like a spinning wheel on the "son fu, son fu" section. Number off the choir 1, 2, 1, 2. Number 1's sing as number 2's listen. Can you hear the spinning wheel? Reverse roles.

O bella fusa

(The Spinning Wheel)

For SATB a cappella

English Text by
MAYNARD KLEIN

By ORLANDO di LASSO (1532-1594)
Edited by MAYNARD KLEIN

129

O OCCHI MANZA MIA (THINE EYES, OH, MY BELOVED)
Composer: Orlando di Lasso (1532-1594), edited by Maynard Klein
Text: Orlando di Lasso, English text by Maynard Klein
Voicing: SATB a cappella

Cultural Context:

Orlando di Lasso lived from 1532-1594 at the end of the time period known as the *Renaissance*. Di Lasso (also known as Lassus) was a notable figure in sixteenth century choral music and was known as the "Belgian Orpheus" as well as the "Prince of Music." He had such a magnificent voice that by the time he was twelve years old he had been kidnapped on three occasions by other churches. He was a composer of international fame, composing Italian *madrigals*, French *chansons*, German *lieder*, and Latin *motets*. He composed over two thousand compositions during his lifetime. To see other examples of di Lasso's work, see "Tutto lo di mi dici 'Canta' " on p. 201 and "O bella fusa" p. 127.

Musical Terms:

andante moderato	*mf* (mezzo forte)	*pp* (pianissimo)
────────── (crescendo)	────────── (decrescendo)	*f* (forte)
poco cresc. (poco crescendo)	*mf* (mezzo forte)	*poco rall.* (poco rallentando)
a tempo	*rall. e dim.* (rallentando e diminuendo)	⌢ₒ (fermata)

Preparation:

Say the words to "O Occhi, manza mia." The capitalized words should be the stressed syllables.

Italian: *O occhi manza mia, cigli dorati!*
Pronunciation: oh oh-kee MAHN-zah MEE-ah chee-LYEE doh-R̃AH-tee

              O faccia d'una luna, stralucenti!
              oh FAH-chee-ah DOO-nah LOO-nah ST̃RAH-loo-CHEHN-tee

              Tiene mi mente, gioia mia bella,
              T(ee)EH-neh mee MEHN-teh JOH-yah MEE-ah BEHL-lah

              guarddam'un poc'a me, a fa mi contiento.
              GWAHR̃-dah-moon POH-kah MEH ah fah MEE kohn-T(ee)EHN-toh

                                      * r̃ = flipped or rolled r.

Evaluation:

In your music, underline the stressed words in your part.
• Speak the Italian words in rhythm.
• Sing your part in Italian remembering the word stress.

O occhi manza mia

(Thine Eyes, Oh, My Beloved)

For SATB a cappella

English text by
MAYNARD KLEIN

By ORLANDO di LASSO (1532-1594)
Edited by MAYNARD KLEIN

SIX FOLK SONGS (I'D ENTER YOUR GARDEN, THE FIDDLER, and HOW SAD FLOW THE STREAMS)
Composer: Johannes Brahms (1833-1897)
Text: German Folk Song, English translation by Harold Heiberg
Voicing: SATB a cappella

Cultural Context:

Johannes Brahms is one of the greatest composers of choral music. A considerable part of Brahms' creative work was devoted to the artful transcription of folk music. He arranged many German folk songs in various ways. The *Six Folk Songs* presented here are Nos. 17-22 in his set of *26 German Folk Songs* (*Deutsche Volkslieder*) for unaccompanied mixed chorus. For more information see p. 149.

Read the words to each verse of the song you are preparing. Are the words meant to be taken literally, or is there a second meaning?

Musical Terms:

I'd Enter Your Garden:	*p* (piano)	———————	(crescendo and decrescendo)
The Fiddler:	*f* (forte)	𝄴 (common time)	5/4
How Sad Flow the Streams:	*p* (piano)	———————	(crescendo and decrescendo)

Preparation:

These songs require special attention to phrasing and stressing held notes within each phrase.

• Study the dynamic markings in the examples below. The ——————— means to keep the energy going across the quarter or dotted quarter.
• Speak the words in rhythm using a noticeable increase in energy across held notes.

"I'd Enter Your Garden":

"The Fiddler":

"How Sad Flow the Streams":

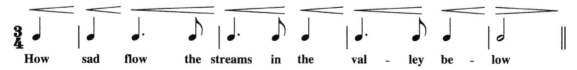

Evaluation:

Evaluate your understanding of notes which require extra energy.

• In your own voice part, mark the held notes which need extra energy like the examples in Preparation.
• After you have learned the pitches and rhythms, sopranos perform a phrase of the song making a noticeable difference on held notes. Other sections listen and evaluate whether the differences were indeed "noticeable."

138

I'd Enter Your Garden

For SATB a cappella

English Translation by
HAROLD HEIBERG

By JOHANNES BRAHMS (1833-1897)
Piano Score Arranged by HERBERT ZIPPER

140

141

The Fiddler

For SATB a cappella

English Translation by
HAROLD HEIBERG

By JOHANNES BRAHMS (1833-1897)
Piano Score Arranged by HERBERT ZIPPER

*Pronounced: mine

back   had   a   hump,   but   his   fid - dling   was   fine.   On   the
prom - ise   to   grant   you   a   worth - i - est   boon.   Play   a
la - dies went danc - ing   a - round   in   a   ring.   When the
fid - dler stood slen - der   and   tall   once   a - gain!   "Oh,   I'll

back   had   a   hump,   but   his   fid - dling   was   fine.   On   the
prom - ise   to   grant   you   a   worth - i - est   boon.   Play   a
la - dies went danc - ing   a - round   in   a   ring.   When the
fid - dler stood slen - der   and   tall   once   a - gain!   "Oh,   I'll

back   had   a   hump,   but   his   fid - dling   was   fine.   On   the
prom - ise   to   grant   you   a   worth - i - est   boon.   Play   a
la - dies went danc - ing   a - round   in   a   ring.   When the
fid - dler stood slen - der   and   tall   once   a - gain!   "Oh,   I'll

back   had   a   hump,   but   his   fid - dling   was   fine.   On   the
prom - ise   to   grant   you   a   worth - i - est   boon.   Play   a
la - dies went danc - ing   a - round   in   a   ring.   When the
fid - dler stood slen - der   and   tall   once   a - gain!   "Oh,   I'll

How Sad Flow the Streams

For SATB a cappella

English Translation by
HAROLD HEIBERG

By JOHANNES BRAHMS (1833-1897)
Piano and Score by HERBERT ZIPPER

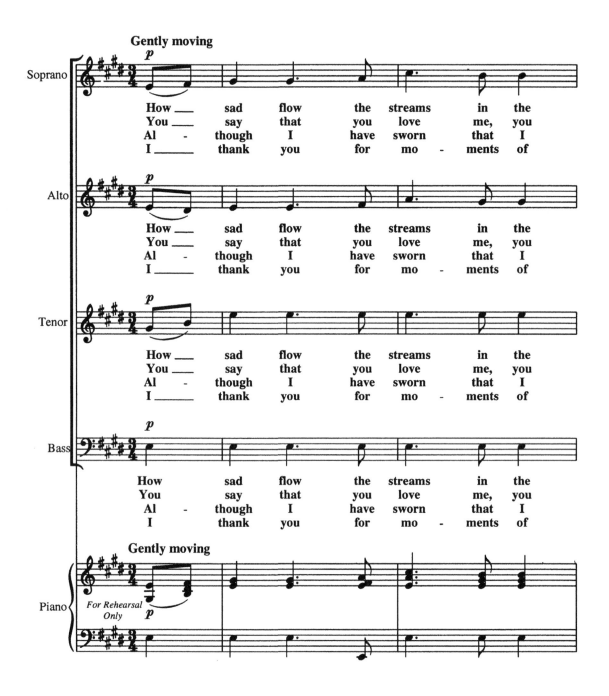

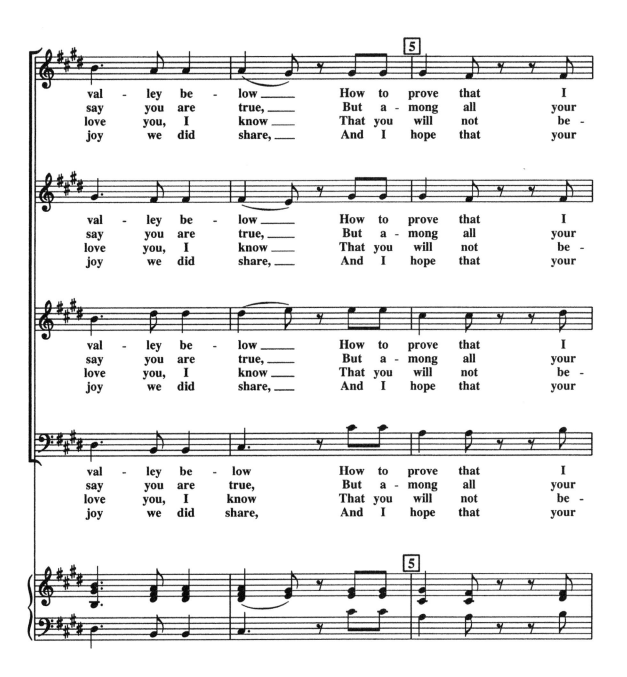

val - ley be - low _____ How to prove that I
say you are true, _____ But a - mong all your
love you, I know _____ That you will not be -
joy we did share, _____ And I hope that your

val - ley be - low _____ How to prove that I
say you are true, _____ But a - mong all your
love you, I know _____ That you will not be -
joy we did share, _____ And I hope that your

val - ley be - low _____ How to prove that I
say you are true, _____ But a - mong all your
love you, I know _____ That you will not be -
joy we did share, _____ And I hope that your

val - ley be - low How to prove that I
say you are true, But a - mong all your
love you, I know That you will not be -
joy we did share, And I hope that your

love   you,   I   nev - er   will   know.
fine   words   are   ly - ing   ones,   too.
lieve   me,   and   so   I   must   go.
luck   will   be   bet - ter   else - where.

love   you,   I   nev - er   will   know.
fine   words   are   ly - ing   ones,   too.
lieve   me,   and   so   I   must   go.
luck   will   be   bet - ter   else - where.

love   you,   I   nev - er   will   know.
fine   words   are   ly - ing   ones,   too.
lieve   me,   and   so   I   must   go.
luck   will   be   bet - ter   else - where.

love   you,   I   nev - er   will   know.
fine   words   are   ly - ing   ones,   too.
lieve   me,   and   so   I   must   go.
luck   will   be   bet - ter   else - where.

SIX FOLK SONGS (AT NIGHT, AWAKE, AWAKE!, and A HOUSE STANDS 'NEATH THE WILLOWS' SHADE)
Composer: Johannes Brahms (1833-1897)
Text: German Folk Song, English translation by Harold Heiberg
Voicing: SATB a cappella

Cultural Context:
Brahms lived and composed during the time known as the *Romantic Period* of music. Characteristics of this period include emotional expression, wide dynamic contrasts, frequent *crescendos* and *decrescendos*, and poems expressing love of nature.

Read the words to each verse of the song you are preparing. Do you understand the poetry well enough to tell the story of what the song is about? Are the words meant to be taken literally, or is there a second meaning? For more information see p. 138.

Musical Terms:

"At Night":

legato

mf (mezzo forte)

f (forte)

> (accent)

———————————— (crescendo and decrescendo)

p (piano)

pp (pianissimo)

"Awake, Awake!":

p (piano)

mf (mezzo forte)

———————————— (crescendo and decrescendo)

cresc. (crescendo)

ritard. (ritardando)

f (forte)

:‖ (repeat sign)

"A House Stands 'Neath the Willows' Shade":

leggiero

♩ (staccato)

> (accent)

f (forte)

p (piano)

cresc. (crescendo)

:‖ (repeat sign)

Preparation:
One of the problems in these three challenging pieces is keeping a sense of legato phrasing while maintaining rhythmic precision. Work on rhythmic precision by pulsing (subdividing) the shortest note value in the song on a neutral syllable.

"At Night":
> The sixteenth note is the shortest note value. Pulse the sixteenth note.

"Awake, Awake!":
> The eighth note is the shortest note value. Pulse the eighth note.

"A House Stands 'Neath the Willows' Shade":
> The sixteenth note is the shortest note value. Pulse the sixteenth note.

Evaluation:
Pulse the remainder of the song without writing in the counts. To do this you will have to know, for example, how many sixteenth notes occur in a dotted eighth note. Notice that the voice parts do not always have the same rhythms.

At Night

For SATB a cappella

English Translation by
HAROLD HEIBERG

By JOHANNES BRAHMS (1833-1897)
Piano and Score Arranged by HERBERT ZIPPER

shad - ows deep, To___ rouse the maid - en___ from her sleep so___ qui - et - ly.
heart to win; Come_ down, my sweet, _and_ let me in so___ qui - et - ly.
be too few To___ tell the love _ I __ feel for you so__ qui - et - ly.

shad - ows deep, To rouse the maid - en___ from her sleep so qui - et - ly.
heart to win; Come down, my sweet, _and_ let me in so qui - et - ly.
be too few To tell the love _ I __ feel for you so qui - et - ly.

shad - ows deep, To rouse the maid - en from her sleep so qui - et - ly.
heart to win; Come down, my sweet, and let me in so qui - et - ly.
be too few To tell the love I feel for you so qui - et - ly.

shad - ows deep, To rouse the maid - en from her sleep so qui - et - ly.
heart to win; Come down, my sweet, and let me in so qui - et - ly.
be too few To tell the love I feel for you so qui - et - ly.

Awake, Awake!

For SATB a cappella

English Translation by
HAROLD HEIBERG

By JOHANNES BRAHMS (1833-1897)
Piano and Score Arranged by HERBERT ZIPPER

154

155

156

A House Stands 'Neath the Willows' Shade

For SATB a cappella

English Translation by
HAROLD HEIBERG

By JOHANNES BRAHMS (1833-1897)
Piano and Score Arranged by HERBERT ZIPPER

wil - lows' shade, With - in it lives a love - ly maid, a
sail - ing by, And sings to me, "My love, good - bye, my
night - in - gale, She tells in song a joy - ous tale, a

shade, With - in it lives a love - ly maid, a
by, And sings to me, "My love, good - bye, my
gale, She tells in song a joy - ous tale, a

wil - lows' shade, With - in it lives a love - ly maid, a
sail - ing by, And sings to me, "My love, good - bye, my
night - in - gale, She tells in song a joy - ous tale, a

shade, With - in it lives a love - ly maid, a
by, And sings to me, "My love, good - bye, my
gale, She tells in song a joy - ous tale, a

love - ly maid. She __ gaz - es up and
love, good - bye!" At __ eve - ning when the
joy - ous tale: You __ too, will build a

love - ly maid. She gaz - es up __ and __
love, good - bye!" At eve - ning when __ the __
joy - ous tale: You too, will build __ a __

love - ly maid. She gaz - es up _____ and
love, good - bye!" At eve - ning when _____ the
joy - ous tale: You too, will build _____ a

love - ly maid. She __ gaz - es up and down the
love, good - bye!" At __ eve - ning when the fire - flies
joy - ous tale: You __ too, will build a nest in

down the   stream,   Oh, where   is   he   of   whom   I   dream? No
fire - flies gleam,   He rows   his   boat   a -   cross   the   stream, So
nest   in   spring,   And on   that   day   this   song   I'll   sing,   "No

down the   stream,   Oh,_ where   is   he   of   whom   I   dream? No
fire - flies gleam,   He_ rows   his   boat   a -   cross   the   stream, So
nest   in   spring,   And_ on   that   day   this   song   I'll   sing,   "No

down the   stream,   Oh,   where_ is__   he   of   whom   I   dream?   No
fire - flies gleam,   He   rows_ his _ boat   a -   cross   the   stream, So
nest   in   spring,   And   on __   that_ day   this   song   I'll   sing,   "No

stream,   Oh, where is   he   of   whom   I __ dream? No   lad more
gleam,   He rows   his   boat   a -   cross   the_ stream,   So   that we
spring,   And on   that   day   this   song   I'll_ sing,   "No   brid - al

160

lad more hand-some sails the Rhine, And he is mine!
that we can to - geth - er be, Just I and he.
brid - al pair was e'er so fine On all the Rhine!"

lad more hand-some sails the_ Rhine, And he is mine!
that we can to - geth - er___ be, Just I and he.
brid - al pair was e'er so _ fine On all the Rhine!"

lad _ more_ hand-some sails the Rhine, And he is mine!
that_ we _ can to - geth - er be, Just I and he.
brid - al ___ pair was e'er so fine On all the Rhine!"

hand - some sails the___ Rhine, And he is mine!
can to - geth - er___ be, Just I and he.
pair was e'er so___ fine On all the Rhine!"

THE SKY CAN STILL REMEMBER

Composer: Michael Gray
Text: Phillips Brooks (1835-1893)
Voicing: SAB

Cultural Context:

Phillips Brooks, who wrote the words to "The Sky Can Still Remember," also wrote the words to "O Little Town of Bethlehem." This particular setting in F-sharp minor features an expressive folk-like melody. Read the text to "The Sky Can Still Remember" as it describes the first Christmas.

Musical Terms:

mp (mezzo piano)   poco   *cresc.* (crescendo)

———————— (decrescendo)   *p* (piano)   *mf* (mezzo forte)

dim. (diminuendo)   *slight ritard.* (slight ritardando)

Preparation:

There are many unison sections in "The Sky Can Still Remember," which will allow you to concentrate on uniformity of tone. Uniformity of tone means that no matter how many singers there are in the choir, the choir still sounds like one voice.

Sing the note below on the sound "oh" (as in measure 23). Begin with one voice and add the others one at a time making sure that the tone sounds like one voice.

Find and rehearse this spot in your music.

Evaluation:

To further concentrate on "uniformity of tone":

• Basses sing the last six measures of "The Sky Can Still Remember," concentrating on uniformity of tone. Other sections listen and evaluate.
• Next, feature the Soprano and Alto section singing their parts separately. Again, other sections should listen and evaluate.

The Sky Can Still Remember

For SAB and Piano

Text by PHILLIPS BROOKS (1835-1893)

Music by MICHAEL A. GRAY

Should be learned in 4/4 but performed in 2/2.

164

Soprano

O, _____ O_ an-gels sweet and splen-did throng

Alto

O an - gels splen-did throng_

Bass

O an - gels_sweet and splen - did throng

in _ our_ hearts and sing Of the won - ders which at -

in our hearts and sing_ of _ the won - ders which at -

in our hearts and sing of the won - ders_which at -

(sweetly)

166

Beth-l'hems hill of bless - ing and find __ the Son of

Beth-l'hems hill __ of bless - ing and __ find the Son of

Beth - l'hems __ hill of bless - ing and find the Son of

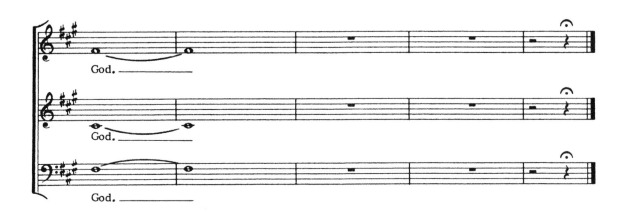

God. _____

God. _____

God. _____

slight rit.

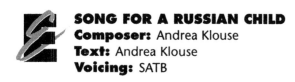

SONG FOR A RUSSIAN CHILD
Composer: Andrea Klouse
Text: Andrea Klouse
Voicing: SATB

Cultural Context:
This beautiful wish for "peace on earth" is a poem to the similarities between American and Russian children. You will recognize the American places mentioned, but the Russian locations may be less familiar. Kyzyl Kum is pronounced "kitzel-koom" and means "red sands." It is a desert lowland located at the Aral-Caspian lowland. Kyzyl Kum is in the very southern part of what used to be the U.S.S.R., but it now lies partly in both Uzbekistan and Kazakhstan.

Kara Sea, pronounced "kahrah" is located at the country's northern-most border with the West Siberian Plain. The sea surrounds three sets of islands (Novaya Zemlya, Franz Josef Land and Severnaya Zemlya). Kara Sea is translated "black sea" and is located in the northern part of Russia.

The American children are standing at the east and west borders of their country (Atlantic and Pacific shores), while the Russian children are singing from the south and north borders of their region. You may want to find these locations on a map.

Musical Terms:

($\downarrow$ =56-63)

——————— (crescendo)

rall. (rallentando)

cresc. (crescendo)

ff (fortissimo)

div. (divisi)

poco rit. (poco ritardando)

——————— (decrescendo)

poco cresc. (poco crescendo)

allargando

molto rit. (molto ritardando)

a tempo

mf (mezzo forte)

f (forte)

con moto

mp (mezzo piano)

Preparation:
Read the words to "Russian Child" before beginning the music.

> *I will sing a song for a Russian child.*
> *It's a song of promise to be.*
> *I will sing a song for a little child, any child whose dreams seem small.*
> *I will reach my hand out to lend a hand.*
> *I will reach my hand across the sea, for the children there are just like you and me.*
>
> *He sings his song from the Kyzyl Kum.*
> *She's singing from Pacific shores.*
> *She sings beside the Kara Sea.*
> *She's singing from the Atlantic.*
> *The song they sing is one of harmony;*
> *Joined strong and rising to a place where hearts and minds are always free!*
>
> *I will sing a song for a Russian child, may he ne'er feel hunger or cold,*
> *While the children sing over all the land, hand in hand, ten thousand bold!*
> *And I'll sing a song for the child at heart in whose land rests all his people's worth,*
> *For the song I sing, for the song they sing is a wish for peace on earth!*

Evaluation:
Write an essay which might serve as an introduction to "Russian Child." You may choose to select one to read during the lengthy introduction to the song. Your essay might include such things as what freedom means to you, what cooperation between countries might mean, or what "peace on earth" truly means.

168

Song for a Russian Child

For SATB and Piano

Words and Music by
ANDREA KLOUSE

172

just like you and me.

just like you and me.

just like you and me.

just like you and me.

B♭m7   D♭/E♭ E♭7 A♭add9   A♭add9/G♭

rall - - - - - - - - -

He sings his song from the Kyz - yl Kum,___

She's sing-ing from Pa-cif - ic

She's sing-ing from Pa-cif - ic

He sings his song from the Kyz - yl Kum,___

mp poco cresc.

mf

mf

mp poco cresc.

28

mp poco cresc.

173

She sings be-side the Kar-a Sea. The song they sing is one of

shores, she's sing-ing from the At - lan - tic. The song they sing is one of

shores, she's sing-ing from the At - lan - tic. The song they sing is one of

She sings be-side the Kar-a Sea. The song they sing is one of

G/D   D7

har - mo-ny; joined strong and ris-ing to a place where hearts and minds are al-ways free!

har - mo-ny; ris-ing to a place where hearts and minds are al-ways free!

har - mo-ny; ris-ing to a place where hearts and minds are al-ways free!

har - mo-ny; ris-ing to a place where hearts and minds are al-ways free!

Gmaj7/B   Em9   E♭   B♭m7   G♭   D♭/F Fm7/E♭ E♭7

174

175

176

178

THREE SPANISH CAROLS (PASTORES Á BELÉN, ¿QUE REGALO?, ADORAR AL NIÑO)
Composer: Traditional Spanish Carols, arranged by Emily Crocker
Text: Traditional Spanish adapted by Jaime Pérez, English text by Emily Crocker
Voicing: SATB a cappella

Cultural Context:

A *carol* is a song of praise or a joyful song of celebration usually related to Christmas time. Occasionally the term is also used for other devotional songs of a joyful character (Easter Carol, May Carol). The name is thought to be derived from the medieval French word "carole," a round dance, performed in celebration of the winter solstice–a ritual later merged with Christmas.

The "Three Spanish Carols" incorporate the traditional story of the shepherds journeying to the manger, bearing gifts, and adoring the newborn Niño (child). This set of three carols was commissioned by the 1991 Texas Choral Directors Association and had its premier performance at the annual TCDA Convention in San Antonio, Texas, that same year.

Musical Terms:

cresc. (crescendo)	poco a poco	*molto rit.* (molto ritardando)
subito	*poco rit.* (poco ritardando)	*a tempo*
divisi	*dim. al fine* (diminuendo al fine)	Presto
accel. e cresc. (accelerando e crescendo)	Più mosso	*fp* (forte piano)
più forte	sempre	*p* (piano)
mp (mezzo piano)	*mf* (mezzo forte)	*f* (forte)

Preparation:

To achieve rhythmic and textual precision, practice the following exercises–first on a neutral syllable and then on the text. Be sure to use crisp beginning consonants, proper pronunciation of the Spanish text, and close the M on the final "tam" in exercise 2. Feel the eighth note pulse in each exercise.

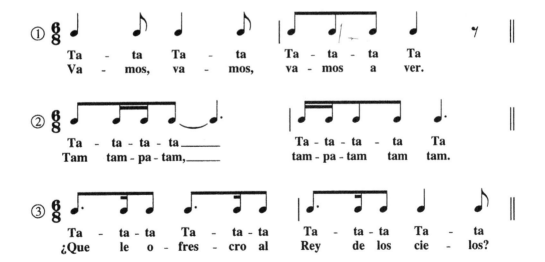

Evaluation:

- Were you able to master all of the different rhythmic patterns in 6/8 time presented in this set of carols?

- How does the Spanish pronunciation compare or differ from other languages you have sung in your choral experience?

Commissioned by the 1991 Texas Choral Directors Association
Glenda Casey, Conductor

Three Spanish Carols

I. Pastores á Belén
(Shepherds, Away)

For SATB a cappella

Spanish Text adapted by JAIME PÉREZ
English Text by EMILY CROCKER

Traditional Spanish Carols
Arranged by EMILY CROCKER

182

183

184

185

II. ¿Que Regalo?
(What Shall I Bring?)

For SATB a cappella

Spanish Text adapted by JAIME PÉREZ
English Text by EMILY CROCKER

Traditional Spanish Carols
Arranged by EMILY CROCKER

*All accompaniment patterns ending in "m" should close immediately to the "m", i.e. "tam-tam-pa-tam (m)".
Keep accompaniment figures very light, and bring out the melodic patterns.

187

*Do not close to "m."

189

190

*Do not close to "m"

III. Adorar al Niño
(Come Adore the Baby)

For SATB a cappella

Spanish Text adapted by JAIME PÉREZ
English Text by EMILY CROCKER

Traditional Spanish Carols
Arranged by EMILY CROCKER

194

195

199

TUTTO LO DI MI DICI "CANTA" (DAY AFTER DAY THEY ALL SAY, "SING")
Composer: Orlando di Lasso (1532-1594), edited by Maynard Klein
Text: Orlando di Lasso, English text by Maynard Klein
Voicing: SATB a cappella

Cultural Context:
Orlando di Lasso lived from 1532 to 1594 at the end the *Renaissance*. He was born in Belgium, but lived in Italy for ten years and spent the last thirty-four years of his life in Germany. Di Lasso was a notable figure in sixteenth century choral music as both a singer and a composer. He composed over two thousand compositions during his lifetime.

"Tutto lo di mi dici 'Canta,' " is an example of a lighter form of Italian vocal writing called a *canzonetta* meaning "little song." Canzonetti were written for *a cappella* singing (voices only) with evenly phrased sections which were often repeated. The text usually was not of a serious nature.

Musical Terms:

allegretto ritmico	*mf* (mezzo forte)	*p* (piano)
f (forte)	*mp* (mezzo piano)	——————— (decrescendo)
——————— (crescendo)	> (accent)	sempre
(fermata)	canzonetta	

Preparation:
To recreate the style that was used during the Renaissance, try these helpful hints:
• Find word phrases which are repeated. Mark them in your music. When singing the repeated phrases, sing with a contrasting dynamic level.
• Staggered entrances occur when different voices begin the same text at different times. Rounds are examples of staggered entrances. Locate the staggered entrances in "Tutto lo di mi dici 'Canta' " that begin with the Italian words:

> "A che tanto cantare?" (mm. 15-16)
> "Voria che mi dicessi" (mm. 19-20)
> "S'io t'haggio" (mm. 51-52)

• Accent the first syllable of "sona" (SOH-nah) each time to make your voices sound like the ringing of a bell. Music of this period was originally notated without barlines. Notice how this section "feels" in three.

Evaluation:
As you rehearse "Tutto lo di mi dici 'Canta,' " check for the following:

• Did I sing the repeated phrases at a different dynamic level?
• Could the staggered entrances be clearly heard?

Continue to check for these elements as you sing Renaissance music. Most students enjoy and experience success singing music of this period.

Tutto lo di mi dici "Canta"
(Day After Day They All Say, "Sing")

For SATB a cappella

English text by
MAYNARD KLEIN

By ORLANDO di LASSO (1532-1594)
Edited by MAYNARD KLEIN

205

207

WHEN I WAS ONE-AND-TWENTY
Composer: Robert Rhein
Text: A.E. Housman (1859-1936)
Voicing: SAB

Cultural Context:
"When I Was One-and-Twenty" is the third song from a collection called *Three Songs from "A Shropshire Lad"* by contemporary composer Robert Rhein. Shropshire is a county in England that is northwest of London and borders Wales.

The well-known English poet and classical scholar A.E. Housman wrote the poetry for the collection. The other poems in the collection are "Loveliest of Trees" and "With Rue My Heart is Laden."

Musical Terms:

mf (mezzo forte) *p subito* (piano subito) *mp* (mezzo piano)

f (forte) *dim.* (diminuendo) ⌢ (fermata)

cresc. (crescendo) *decresc.* (decrescendo)

Preparation:
Use very round and tall vowel sounds when singing "When I Was One-and-Twenty." Singing with tall, uniform vowels will help improve your choir's tone and diction.

• Practice saying the words below as indicated.

when = whehn	was = wahs	one = wahn
a = ah	away = ah-WEH(ee)	I = ah(ee)
to = too	again = ah-GEHN	the = thah
of = ahv	rue = roo	true = troo
crowns = KRAH(oo)ns	pounds = PAH(oo)nds	

• Find the words listed above in your music and circle them as a reminder to sing with tall, round vowels.

Evaluation:
Read the text of "When I Was One-and-Twenty." What is the poet saying? Write a short essay explaining the meaning of the words from your point of view.

For Mia Durham

When I Was One-and-Twenty

For SAB and Piano

Text by A.E. HOUSMAN (1859-1936)

Music by ROBERT RHEIN

(no breath)

crowns and pounds and guin - eas But not your heart a - way; Give

(no breath)

crowns and pounds and guin - eas But not your heart a - way;____ Give

(no breath)

crowns and pounds and guin - eas But not your heart a - way; Give

pearls a - way and ru - bies But keep your fan - cy free." But

pearls a - way and ru - bies But keep your fan - cy free." But____

pearls a - way and ru - bies But keep your fan - cy free." ____ But

211

212

213

214

WITH A VOICE OF SINGING
Composer: Martin Shaw
Text: Psalm text adapted by Martin Shaw
Voicing: SATB

Cultural Context:
Martin Shaw was a prolific composer of sacred music. "With a Voice of Singing," written in 1923 for a church choir festival, is probably his most famous work. It is often sung by both church choirs and school choirs for its sense of majesty and joy.

"With a Voice of Singing" is made up of two styles of writing: *polyphonic* and *homophonic*. In polyphonic writing, each voice part enters at a different time; therefore, different voices are singing different words at the same time. In homophonic writing, each part may have different notes, but every person is singing the same words at the same time. All parts should be rhythmically together when singing the homophonic sections. Emphasize each individual entrance in the polyphonic sections.

Musical Terms:

(♩ = ca. 144)	*f* (forte)	*mf* (mezzo forte)
p (piano)	———————— (crescendo)	*div.* (divisi)
ff (fortissimo)	Unis. (unison)	*poco rit.* (poco ritardando)
a tempo	*cresc.* (crescendo)	allargando
mp (mezzo piano)	homophonic	polyphonic

Preparation:
To prepare for singing both polyphonic and homophonic sections, do the following:

1. Mark an "H" in your music where each homophonic section starts.
2. Mark a "P" in your music where each polyphonic section starts.

Evaluation:
To demonstrate that you are able to perform polyphonic and homophonic sections appropriately, record your choir singing this piece. As you listen to the recording, answer the following questions:

- Was the choir precisely together in the homophonic sections?
- Was a single voice or a single section too loud?
- Was each entrance heard in the polyphonic sections?
- Was one voice part louder than the others in the polyphonic sections?

Dedicated to G. Hylton Stewart
Composed for the 1923 Annual Festival of the Rochester Diocesan Church Choirs Association

With A Voice Of Singing

For SATB and Piano

Psalm text adapted by
MARTIN SHAW

By MARTIN SHAW

ia.   De-clare ye

ia.   De-clare ye this,   de -

ia.   De-clare ye this,   de - clare, de-clare ye

ia. De-clare ye this,   and let   it be heard, de-clare ye

senza Ped.

this,   and let it be   heard, Al - le - lu -   -

clare   and let it be   heard, Al - le - lu -   -

this, de-clare and let   it be heard, Al - le - lu -   -

this, de-clare and let   it be heard, Al - le - lu -   -

Ped.

217

Lord hath de - liv - er-ed his peo - ple, Al - le -

Lord hath de - liv - er-ed his peo - ple, Al -

Lord hath de - liv - er-ed his peo - ple,

Lord hath de - liv - er-ed his peo - ple,

lu - ia. The Lord hath de -

- le - lu - ia. The Lord hath de -

Al - le - lu - ia. The Lord hath de -

Al - le - lu - ia. The Lord hath de -

O be joy-ful in God, all ye lands,

O sing prais-es to the hon-or of his

name, make his praise to be glo -

name, make his praise to be glo -

name, make his praise to be glo -

name, make his praise to be glo -

- rious.

- rious.

- rious.

- rious.

223

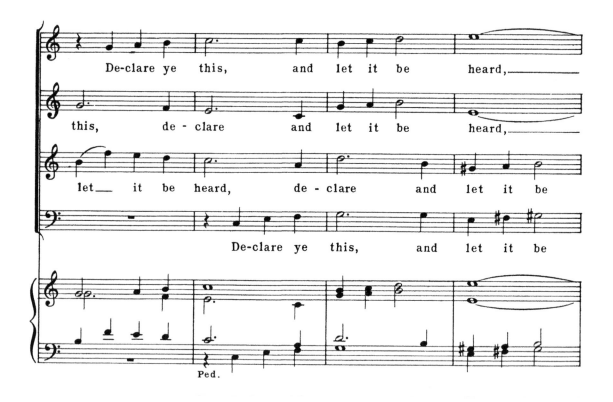

De-clare ye this, and let it be heard,_____

this, de - clare and let it be heard,_____

let__ it be heard, de - clare and let it be

De-clare ye this, and let it be

Ped.

poco rit.

__ Al - le - lu - ia.__

__ Al - le - lu - ia.__

heard, Al - le - lu - ia.__

heard, Al - le - lu - ia.__

Full Sw.

poco rit.

224

225

GLOSSARY

a cappella [It.] (ah-kah-PEH-lah) - Singing without instrumental accompaniment.

ad libitum, ad lib. [Lat.] (ahd LEE-bee-toom) - "At will." The performer may improvise freely, omit a part, or vary the tempo.

accelerando (*accel.*) [It.] (ahk-chel-leh-RAHN-doh) - Becoming faster; a gradual increase in tempo.

accent ($\overset{>}{}$) - Stress or emphasize a note (or chord) over others around it. Accents occur by singing the note louder or stressing the beginning consonant or vowel.

accidentals - Symbols that move the pitch up or down a half step.

    - sharp (♯) - raises the pitch one half step.
    - flat (♭) - lowers the pitch one half step.
    - natural (♮) - cancels a previous *sharp* or *flat*. (When it cancels a flat, the pitch is raised one half step; when it cancels a sharp, the pitch is lowered one half step).
    Accidentals affect all notes of the same pitch that follow the accidental within the same measure, or if an altered note is *tied* over a *barline*.

adagio [It.] (ah-DAH-jee-oh) - Tempo marking indicating slow.

al fine [It.] (ahl FEE-neh) - To ending. An indicator following *D.C.* or *D.S.*. From the Latin *finis*, "to finish."

allargando (*allarg.*) [It.] (ahl-lahr-GAHN-doh) - Broadening, becoming slower, sometimes with an accompanying *crescendo*.

allegretto [It.] (ahl-leh-GRET-toh) - A light, cheerful, fast tempo; a bit slower than *allegro*.

allegro [It.] (ah-LEH-groh) - Tempo marking indicating fast.

alto - A treble voice that is lower than the *soprano*, usually written in the *treble clef*.

andante [It.] (ahn-DAHN-teh) - Tempo marking indicating medium or "walking" tempo.

animato (or animoso) [It.] (ah-nee-MAH-toh) - Style marking meaning animated.

arranger - The person who takes an already existing composition and reorganizes it to fit a new instrumentation or voicing.

articulation - The clear pronunciation of text using the lips, teeth, and tongue. The singer must attack consonants crisply and use proper vowel formation.

a tempo - Return to the original tempo.

ballad - A narrative song dealing with dramatic episodes; a simpler, sentimental song; an air. Many ballads have been passed down orally for generations.

balletto [It.] (bah-LEH-toh) - A 16th century vocal composition with dance-rhythms, often including phrases of nonsense syllables like "fa-la-la." Giovanni Gastoldi wrote the earliest known collection of balletti.

bar - See *measure*.

barline - A vertical line that divides the staff into smaller sections called measures. A double barline indicates the end of a section or piece of music.

Barline   Double Barline

Baroque Period (ca. 1600-1750) (bah-ROHK) - The period in Western music history that extended from 1600 to about 1750; also the musical styles of that period. The style features of most Baroque music include frequent use of *polyphony*; fast, motor-like rhythms; and use of the *chorale*. Some famous Baroque composers were Johann Sebastian Bach, George Frideric Handel, and Antonio Vivaldi.

bass - A male voice written in *bass clef* that is lower than a *tenor* voice.

bass clef - The symbol at the beginning of the staff used for lower voices and instruments, and the piano left hand. It generally refers to pitches lower than *middle C*. The two dots are on either side of F, so it is often referred to as the F clef.

beat - The unit of recurring pulse in music.

ben [It.] (bān) - Well, good.

blue notes - Notes found in the *blues* scale which give it a unique sound. They are the flatted third and flatted seventh *scale* degrees of the *major* scale. Authentic blue notes are not exactly a flatted third or seventh, but fall somewhere in between the regular third (or seventh) and the flatted third (or seventh). See also *blues*.

blues - One of America's unique contributions to Western music. The blues is a style of music that has origins in early twentieth century African-American cultures. It combines elements of *syncopation, blue notes,* and many elements found in *spirituals* of the early American slaves. See also *blue notes*.

breath mark (˒) - An indicator within a phrase or melody where the musician should breathe. See also *no breath* and *phrase marking*.

brio [It.] (BREE-oh) - Vigor, spirit.

caesura (//) [Fr.] (seh-SHOO-rah) - A break or pause between two musical phrases. Also called a *break*.

call and response - Alternation between two performers or groups of performers. Often used in *spirituals*, this technique begins with a leader (or group) singing a phrase followed by a response of the same phrase (or continuation of the phrase) by a second group.

canon - A musical form in which a melody in one part is followed a short time later by other parts performing the same melody. Canons are sometimes called *rounds*.

cantata [It.] (cahn-TAH-tah) - A large work (originally sacred) involving solos, chorus, organ, and occasionally orchestra. The cantata tells a story through text and music. Johann Sebastian Bach wrote a cantata for each Sunday of the church year.

canzonetta [It.] (kahn-zoh-NEH-tah) - A light vocal piece (from the Italian "little song") popular in Italy during the mid-1500s. Similar vocal styles appeared in England and Germany in the 1500s and 1600s. Canzonetti originally contained many stanzas and were *homophonic* in structure.

chanson [Fr.] (shan-sawn) - A French term in use since the middle ages describing a wide range of poetry and song. The troubadour (traveling minstrel) cultivated and developed the chanson. It later took a *polyphonic* form which naturally influenced and was itself influenced by the Italian *madrigal*. See also lied and *madrigal*.

chantey - A song sung by sailors in rhythm with their work.

chorale - A congregational song or hymn originally created in the German Protestant Church. It was a very popular source for compositions, especially during the Baroque Period with composers such as Johann Sebastian Bach.

chord - Three or more pitches sounding at the same time or in succession as in a broken chord. See also *interval*.

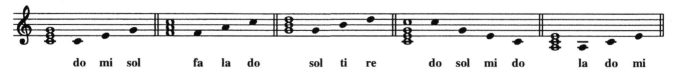

do	mi	sol		fa	la	do		sol	ti	re		do	sol	mi	do		la	do	mi

chorus - See *refrain*.

chromatic - Moving up or down by half steps, often outside of the key. Also the name of a *scale* composed entirely of half steps (all twelve pitches within an *octave*). The chromatic scale is distinct from the *diatonic* scale.

Classical Period (ca. 1750-1835) - The period in Western music history beginning in Italy in 1750 and continuing until about 1825. Music of the Classical Period emphasized balance of phrase and structure. Ludwig von Beethoven, Wolfgang Amadeus Mozart, and Joseph Haydn were famous composers from the Classical Period.

clef - The symbol at the beginning of the staff that identifies a set of pitches. See also *bass clef* and *treble clef*.

coda (⊕) [It.] (COH-dah) - Ending. A concluding portion of a composition.

common time (₵) - Another name for the meter ⁴⁄₄. See also *cut time*.

composer - The writer or creator of a song or musical composition. See also *arranger*.

compound meter - Meters which have a multiple of 3 such as 6 or 9 (but not 3 itself). Compound meter reflects the note that receives the division unlike *simple meter*. (Ex. ⁶⁄₈ = six divisions to the beat in two groups of three where the eighth note receives one division.) An exception to the compound meter rule is when the music occurs at a slow tempo, then the music is felt in beats rather than divisions. See also *meter* and *time signature*.

con [It.] (kohn) - With.

crescendo (*cresc.* or ⟍⟋) [It.] (kreh-SHEN-doh) - Gradually growing louder. The opposite of *decrescendo*.

cued notes - Smaller notes indicating either *optional harmony* or notes from another voice part.

cut time (₵) - ²⁄₂ time, the half note gets the beat.

da capo (D.C.) [It.] (dah KAH-poh) - Repeat from the beginning. See also *dal segno* and *al fine*.

dal segno (D.S.) [It.] (dahl SEHN-yoh) - Go back to the sign (𝄋) and repeat.

D.C. al fine [It.] - Repeat from the beginning to *fine* or end. See also *da capo* and *al fine*.

decrescendo (*decresc.* or ⟋⟍) [It.] (deh-kreh-SHEN-doh) - Gradually growing softer. The opposite of *crescendo*. See also *diminuendo*.

descant - A high ornamental voice part often lying above the melody.

diatonic - Step by step movement within a regular *scale* (any key). A combination of the seven whole and half steps (of different pitch names) within a key. Distinct from *chromatic*.

diminuendo (*dim.*) [It.] (dih-min-new-EN-doh) - Gradually growing softer. See also *decrescendo*.

diphthong (DIF-thong) - A combination of two vowel sounds consisting of a primary vowel sound and a secondary vowel sound. The secondary vowel sound is (usually) at the very end of the diphthong. (Ex. The word "I" is really a diphthong using an "ah" and an "ee." The "ee" is a very brief sound at the end of the word.)

divisi (div.) [It.] (dee-VEE-see) - Divide; the parts divide.

dolce [It.] (DOHL-cheh) - Sweetly; usually soft as well.

dotted barline - A "helper" *barline* in songs with unusual *time signatures* such as 5/8 and 7/8. The dotted barline helps divide the measure into two or more divisions of *triple* or *duple* beat groups.

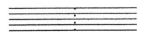

downbeat - The accented first beat of the measure.

D.S. al Coda [It.] (ahl KOH-dah) - Repeat from the sign (𝄋) and sing the *coda* when you see the symbol (⊕).

D.S. al fine [It.] (ahl FEE-neh) - Repeat from the sign (𝄋) to *fine* or ending.

duple - Any *time signature* or group of beats that is a multiple of 2.

dynamic - The loudness or softness of a line of music. Dynamic changes may occur frequently within a composition.

endings - (First and second endings) Alternate endings to a repeated section.

enharmonic - Identical tones which are named and written differently. For instance, F♯ and G♭ are the same note, they are "enharmonic" with each other.

ensemble - A group of musicians (instrumentalists, singers, or some combination) who perform together.

espressivo [It.] (es-pres-SEE-voh) - Expressive, emotional.

esuberante [It.] (eh-zoo-beh-RAHN-teh) - exuberant, high-spirited, or lively.

fermata (⌢) [It.] (fur-MAH-tah) - Hold the indicated note (or rest) for longer than its value; the length is left up to the interpretation of the director or the performer.

fine [It.] (FEE-neh) - Ending. From the Latin *finis*, "to finish."

flat (♭) - An *accidental* that lowers the pitch of a note one half step. Flat also refers to faulty intonation when the notes are sung or played sightly under the correct pitch.

form - The design and structure of a composition or section of a composition.

forte (𝑓) [It.] (FOR-teh) - Loud.

fortissimo (𝑓𝑓) [It.] (for-TEE-see-moh) - Very loud.

freely - A style marking permitting liberties with tempo, dynamics, and style. *Rubato* may also be incorporated.

fuoco [It.] (foo-OH-coh) - Fire.

galliard (gahl-LYARD) - A lively 16th century dance in triple time.

giocoso [It.] (joh-KOH-soh) - Humorous.

grand staff - A grouping of two staves.

grazioso [It.] (grah-tzee-OH-soh) - Graceful or delicate.

half step - The smallest distance (or *interval*) between two notes on a keyboard. Shown symbolically (**v**). The *chromatic* scale is composed entirely of half steps.

half time - See *cut time*.

harmonic interval - *Intervals* played simultaneously.

harmony - Two or more musical tones sounding simultaneously.

hemiola [Gr.] (hee-mee-OH-lah) - A unique rhythmical device in which the beat of a *triple meter* has the feeling of *duple meter* (or the reverse) regardless of *barlines* and *time signatures*. This is accomplished through *ties* and/or *accent* placement.

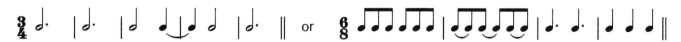

homophony [Gr.] (haw-MAW-faw-nee) - Music in which melodic interest is concentrated in one voice part and may have subordinate accompaniment (distinct from *polyphony* in which all voice parts are equal). Homophony is also music which consists of two or more voice parts with similar or identical rhythms. From the Greek words meaning "same sounds," homophony could be described as being "hymn-style."

hushed - A style marking indicating a soft, whispered tone.

interval - The distance between two pitches.

intonation - Accuracy of pitch.

key - The organization of tonality around a single pitch (*key-note*). See also *key-note* and *key signature*.

key-note - The pitch which is the tonal center of a key. The first tone (note) of a scale. It is also called the *tonic*. A key is named after the key-note; for example in the key of A♭, A♭ is the key-note. See also *key* and *key signature*.

key signature - The group of *sharps* or *flats* at the beginning of a staff which combine to indicate the locations of the key-note and configuration of the *scale*. If there are no sharps or flats, the key is automatically C major or A minor.

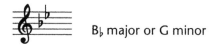 B♭ major or G minor

legato [It.] (leh-GAH-toh) - Smooth and connected. Opposite of *staccato*.

ledger lines (or leger lines) - The short lines used to extend the lines and spaces of the *staff.*

230

leggiero [It.] (leh-JEE-roh) - Light articulation; sometimes non-*legato*.

lento [It.] (LEHN-toh) - Slow.

lied [Ger. pl. Lieder] (leet; LEE-dehr) - In German, a musical term applying to any song. By the middle 1800s the lied developed into what has later been termed the artsong—a composition in which composers combined poetry and voice with piano accompaniment to create a new musical expression. See also chanson and *madrigal*.

loco [It.] (LOH-koh) - "Place." Return to the normal place (usually after playing one or more octaves above or below written pitch).

macaronic text - Text in which two languages are used (usually Latin and one other language).

madrigal - A kind of 16th century Italian composition based on secular poetry. Madrigals were popular into the 17th century.

maestoso [It.] (mah(ee)-STOH-soh) - Majestic.

major key/scale/mode - A specific arrangement of whole steps and half steps in the following order:

Letter Names:	G	A	B	C	D	E	F♯	G
Moveable Do:	do	re	mi	fa	sol	la	ti	do
Fixed Do:	sol	la	ti	do	re	mi	fi	sol
Numbers:	1	2	3	4	5	6	7	1

See also *minor key/scale/mode*.

marcato [It.] (mahr-KAH-toh) - Marked or stressed, march-like.

mass - The central religious service of the Roman Catholic Church. It consists of several sections divided into two groups: Proper of the Mass (text changes for every day) and Ordinary of the Mass (text stays the same in every mass). Between the years 1400 and 1600 the mass assumed its present form consisting of the Kyrie, Gloria, Credo, Sanctus, and Agnus Dei. It may include chants, hymns, and psalms as well. The mass also developed into large musical works for chorus, soloists, and even orchestra.

measure - A group of beats divided by *barlines*. Measures are sometimes called *bars*. The first beat of each measure is usually accented.

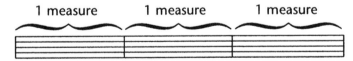

melisma - Long groups of notes sung on one syllable of text.

melodic interval - Notes that comprise an *interval* played in succession.

melody - A succession of musical tones; also the predominant line in a song.

meno [It.] (MEH-noh) - Less.

meter - A form of rhythmic organization (grouping of beats). The kind of meter designated by the *time signature*. See also *simple* and *compound meters*.

meter signature - See *time signature*.

metronome marking - A marking which appears over the top staff of music which indicates the kind of note which will get the beat, and the number of beats per minute as measured by a metronome. It reveals the *tempo*. (Ex. (♩ = 100)).

mezzo forte (*mf*) [It.] (MEH-tsoh FOR-teh) - Medium loud.

mezzo piano (*mp*) [It.] (MEH-tsoh pee-AH-noh) - Medium soft.

middle C - The C which is located closest to the middle of the piano keyboard. Middle C can be written in either the *treble* or *bass clef*.

minor key/scale/mode - A specific arrangement of whole steps and half steps in the following order:

Letter Names:	D	E	F	G	A	B♭	C	D
Moveable La:	la	ti	do	re	mi	fa	sol	la
Fixed La:	re	mi	fa	sol	la	te	do	re
Numbers:	1	2	3	4	5	6	7	1

See also *major key/scale/mode*.

mixed meter - Frequently changing meters or *time signatures* within a piece of music.

moderato [It.] (mah-deh-RAH-toh) - Moderate tempo.

modulation - Changing keys within a song. Adjust to the *key signature*, the *key-note*, and proceed.

molto [It.] (MOHL-toh) - Much, very. (Ex. molto rit. = greatly slowing)

monophony - Music which consists of a single melody. This earliest form of composition is from the Greek words meaning "one sound." Chant or *plainsong* is monophony.

morendo [It.] (moh-REHN-doh) - Fading away.

mosso [It.] (MOH-soh) - Moved, agitated.

motet (moh-teht) - A major type of musical composition from the 1200s into the 1700s. The motet went through many different forms and developments beginning with the simpler medieval motet and progressing to the more intricate *Renaissance* motet which is generally considered a *polyphonic* setting of sacred Latin text.

moto [It.] (MOH-toh) - Motion.

mysterioso [It.] (mih-steer-ee-OH-soh) - A style marking indicating a mysterious or haunting mood.

natural (♮) - Cancels a previous *sharp* (♯) or *flat* (♭). (When it cancels a flat, the pitch is raised one half step; when it cancels a sharp, the pitch is lowered one half step.)

no breath (♩ ♩ or N.B.) - An indication by either the *composer/arranger* or the editor of where *not* to breathe in a line of music. See also *phrase marking*.

notation - All written notes and symbols which are used to represent music.

octave - The *interval* between two notes of the same name. Octaves can be indicated within a score using 𝄞𝄞 (octave above) and 𝄞𝄞 (octave below).

ost1 octave

ostinato [It.] (ah-stee-NAH-toh) - A repeated pattern used as a harmonic basis.

optional divisi (opt. div.) [It.] (dee-VEE-see) - The part splits into optional harmony. The smaller sized *cued notes* indicate the optional notes to be used.

pastoral - Subject matter pertaining to nature (outdoor) scenes.

phrase marking (⌒‾‾‾‾‾) - An indication by either the *composer* or the *arranger* as to the length of a line of music or melody. This marking often means that the musician is not to breathe during its duration. See also *no breath*.

piano (*p*) [It.] (pee-AH-noh) - Soft.

pianissimo (*pp*) [It.] (pee-ah-NEE-see-moh) - Very soft.

pick-up - An incomplete measure at the beginning of a song or phrase.

pitch - The highness or lowness of musical sounds.

più [It.] (pew) - More. (Ex. più forte or più mosso allegro)

plainsong - An ancient liturgical (sacred) chant–a single melody line with free rhythm sung *a cappella.*

poco [It.] (POH-koh) - Little. (Ex. poco cresc. = a little crescendo)

poco a poco [It.] (POH-koh ah POH-koh) - Little by little (Ex. poco a poco cresc. = increase in volume, little by little)

polyphony [Gr.] (paw-LIH-faw-nee) - Music which consist of two or more independent melodies which combine to create simultaneous voice parts with different rhythms. Polyphony often involves contrasting dynamics and imitation from part to part. From the Greek words meaning "many sounds," polyphony is sometimes called counterpoint.

presto [It.] (PREH-stoh) - Very fast.

rallentando (*rall.*) [It.] (rahl-en-TAHN-doh) - Gradually slower. See also *ritardando.*

refrain - Refers to a section of a song with both textual and musical repetition. This section is also called *chorus* since it is perfomed by the full chorus of singers, whereas a soloist performs the verses (or stanzas).

relative major/minor - Major and minor tonalities which share the same *key signature.*

G major   E minor

233

Renaissance Period (ca. 1450-1600) (REHN-neh-sahns) - A period in the Western world following the Middle Ages. Renaissance means "rebirth" and was a celebration of entrance into the modern age of thought and invention. In music it was a period of great advancement in notation and compositional ideas. *Polyphony* was developing and the *madrigal* became popular. Orlando di Lasso, Giovanni da Palestrina, Tomás Luis de Victoria, and Josquin Des Prez were some of the more famous Renaissance composers.

repeat sign (‖: :‖) - Repeat the section. If the repeat sign is omitted, go back to the beginning. See also *endings*.

resolution (res.) - A progression from a dissonant tone or harmony to a consonant harmony. (Usually approached by step.) See also *suspension*.

rhythm - The organization of non-pitched sounds in time. Rhythm encompasses note and rest duration as well as *meters*, *tempos*, and their relationships.

ritardando (*rit.*) [It.] (ree-tahr-DAHN-doh) - Gradually slower. See also *rallentando*.

ritmico [It.] (riht-MEE-koh) - Rhythmic.

Romantic Period (ca. 1825-1900) - A period in 19th century Western art, literature, and music that lasted into the early 20th century. In music, as well as the other areas, Romanticism focused on the emotion of art. Works from this period emphasized the emotional effect music has on the listener through dynamic contrasts and different ways of changing the "mood." Opera flourished as well as chamber music. Some famous Romantic composers are Franz Schubert, Frederick Chopin, Hector Berlioz, Johannes Brahms, and Richard Wagner.

root tone - The lowest note of a *triad* in its original position; the note on which the chord is built and named.

round - see *canon*.

rubato [It.] (roo-BAH-toh) - The tempo is free, left up to the interpretation of the director or performer.

scale - An inventory or collection of pitches. The word "scale" (from the Italian *scala*) means ladder. Thus, many musical scales are a succession of pitches higher and lower.

score - The arrangement of a group of vocal and instrumental staffs which all sound at the same time.

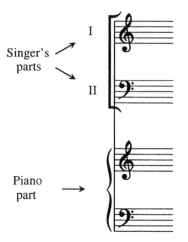

sempre [It.] (SEHM-preh) - Always , continually. (Ex. sempre forte = always loud)

senza [It.] (SEHN-tsah) - Without.

sequence - The successive repetition of a short melodic idea at different pitch levels.

sequence

sforzando (sfz) [It.] (sfor-TSAHN-doh) - A strong accent on a note.

sharp (♯) - An *accidental* that raises the pitch of a note one half step. Also, faulty intonation in which the note is sung slightly above the correct pitch.

sign (𝄋 or Segno) [It.] (SEHN-yoh) - A symbol that marks the place in music where the musician is to skip back to from the *dal Segno* (*D.S.*).

simile (*sim.*) [It.] (SIM-eh-lee) - Continue the same way.

simple meter - Meters which are based upon the note which receives the beat. (Ex. ⁴⁄₄ or 𝄴 is based upon the quarter note receiving the beat.)

skip - The melodic movement of one note to another in *intervals* larger than a step.

slide (𝅘) - To approach a note from underneath the designated pitch and "slide" up to the correct pitch. Slides often appear in jazz, pop tunes, and *spirituals*.

slur (𝅘) - A curved line placed above or below a group of notes to indicate that they are to be sung on the same text syllable. Slurs are also used in instrumental music to indicate that the group of notes should be performed *legato* (smoothly connected).

solfège [Fr.] (SOHL-fehj) - The study of sight-singing using pitch syllables (do re mi, etc.).

solo [It., Lat., Sp.] (SOH-loh) - "Alone." To perform alone or as the predominant part.

soprano - The highest treble voice, usually written in *treble clef.*

sostenuto [It.] (sohs-teh-NOO-toh) - Sustained.

spirito [It.] (SPEE-ree-toh) - Spirit.

spiritual - Religious folk songs of African American origin associated with work, recreation, or religious gatherings. They developed prior to the Civil War and are still influential today. They have a strong rhythmic character and are often structured in *call and response.*

spoken - Reciting text with the speaking voice rather than singing the designated line. Often indicated with ⨉ instead of notes.

staccato (𝅘) [It.] (stah-KAH-toh) - Short, separated notes. Opposite of *legato.*

staff - The five horizontal parallel lines and four spaces between them on which notes are placed to show *pitch*. The staff can be extended by using *ledger lines.*

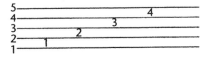

The lines and spaces are numbered from the bottom up.

stagger breathing - A choral performance technique where each singer breathes in a different place within an extended phrase or held note, thus achieving an uninterrupted stream of sound from the choir.

step - Melodic movement from one note to the next higher or lower *scale* degree.

strophe - A strophe is a verse or stanza in a song. If a song has many verses it is said to be strophic.

style marking - An indicator at the beginning of a song or section of song which tells the musician, in general, what style the music should be performed. (Ex. *freely* or *animato*)

subito (*sub.*) [It.] (SOO-bee-toh) - Suddenly. (Ex. sub. piano = suddenly soft)

suspension (sus.) - The sustaining or "suspending" of a pitch from a consonant chord into a dissonant chord often using a *tie*. The resulting dissonant chord then *resolves* to a consonant chord. The musical effect is one of tension and release. See also *resolution*.

swing - A change in interpretation of eighth note durations in some music (often jazz and *blues*). Groups of two eighth notes (♫) are no longer sung evenly, instead they are performed like part of a *triplet* ($\overline{}^{3}$ ♩♪). The eighth notes still appear ♫ . A swing style is usually indicated at the beginning of a song or section (♫ = $\overline{}^{3}$♩♪).

syllables - Names given to pitch units or rhythm units to aid in sight-reading.

syncopation - The use of *accents* and *ties* to create rhythmic interest. The result is a rhythmic pattern which stresses notes on the off beat. This technique is commonly found in *spirituals* and jazz.

tempo - The speed of the beat.

tempo I - Return to the first tempo. Also called tempo primo.

tenor - A male voice written in *bass clef* or *treble clef*. It is lower than the *alto*, but higher than the *bass*.

tenuto ($\bar{\rho}$) [It.] (teh-NOO-toh) - A slight stress on the indicated note. The note is held for its full value.

terraced dynamics - A technique commonly found in *Baroque* music in which dynamic changes are made suddenly (for example *p* (piano) and suddenly *f* (forte)).

texture - The interrelationship of the voices and/or instruments within a piece of music. *Monophonic*, *homophonic*, and *polyphonic* are all types of textures.

tie (⌢) - A line connecting two or more notes of the same pitch so that their durations are their combined sum. Ties often occur over *barlines*.

time signature - The symbol placed at the beginning of a composition or section to indicate its meter. This most often takes the form of a fraction ($\frac{4}{4}$ or $\frac{3}{4}$), but may also involve a symbol as in the case of common time (C) and cut time (¢). The upper number indicates the number of beats in a measure and the lower number indicates which type of note receives the beat. (An exception occurs in *compound meters*. See *compound meter* for an explanation.)

to coda - Go to the ⊕ .

tonality - The organization of *pitches* in a song in which a certain pitch (tone) is designated as the *key-note* or the note which is the tonal center of a *key*.

tone - A musical sound of definite pitch and quality.

tonic - The *key-note* of a key or scale.

tonic chord - The name given to the chord built on the *key-note* of the scale.

transpose - To rewrite or perform a song in a *key* other than the original.

treble clef - The symbol at the beginning of the staff used for higher voices and instruments, and the piano right hand. It generally refers to pitches higher then *middle C*. The curve is wrapped around the G, as a result it is also called the G clef.

triad - A special type of 3-note chord built in 3rds over a *root tone*.

trill (*tr* ~~~~) - Rapid alteration (within a key) between the marked note and the one above it.

triple - Any *time signature* or group of beats that is a multiple of 3.

triplet - A borrowed division of the beat where three notes of equal duration are to be sung in the time normally occupied by two notes of equal duration. Usually indicated with a 3.

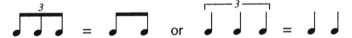

tutti [It.] (TOOT-tee) - "All." Term used for entrance of the full ensemble.

unison (unis.) - All parts singing the same notes at the same time (or singing in *octaves*).

villancico [Sp.] (vee-yahn-SEE-koh or bee-yahn-SEE-koh) - A composition of Spanish origin from the 15th and 16th centuries. Similar to the *madrigal*, this type of work is based on secular poetry and is structured around the verses and refrains of its text.

vivace [It.] (vee-VAH-cheh) - Very fast.

whole step - The combination of two successive half steps. Shown symbolically (⊔).

 **TO THE TEACHER**

Why We Wrote This Book

We created this series because we are vitally committed to the nurturing of choral music, to the more effective teaching of choral music, and particularly to the encouragement of the young musicians who perform choral music. We believe that every child is musically expressive and deserves the opportunity to explore that capacity.

Too often, our definitions of literacy have been limited to words on paper. Although aspects of music can be taught as the written word (i.e., as a series of facts or as a written symbolic language), ultimately music is best understood not through the written word, but rather as a unique way of looking at the world, a special dimension of human understanding. What one understands, expresses, or feels when performing choral music is indeed "another way of knowing." We believe that it is vital that our children be given opportunities to experience this expanded literacy.

Janice Killian   **Michael O'Hern**   **Linda Rann**

About the Series

The four levels of *Essential Repertoire* (Young Choir, Developing Choir, Concert Choir, and Concert Choir - Artist Level) contain choral literature especially selected for choirs of differing ages and experience levels.

Level II, *Essential Repertoire for the Developing Choir*, contains selections which take into account the characteristics of the adolescent voice. It contains musically accessible pieces which would be ideal for the beginning of the year, as well as selections appropriate for later in the year, or for groups which are ready for a special challenge. *Essential Repertoire for the Developing Choir* is specifically designed for ninth and tenth graders, but the material included might be appropriate for any chorus, regardless of age.

Features of the Program

Each repertoire book contains a wide range of literature:

- a variety of historical periods
- a variety of other countries and cultures
- a mixture of English and foreign-language texts
- a variety of challenging and beginning level songs
- a mixture of styles: masterworks, folksongs and spirituals; a cappella and accompanied pieces; sacred and secular works; arrangements of familiar songs; and a few pop-style selections

Every effort was made to select high quality, time-tested literature.

Each song is independent of the others, i.e. there is no special sequence intended. Little prior knowledge is assumed on the part of the student. Teachers are encouraged to make selections as needed to create a varied and meaningful classroom and concert program.

Student information pages are included with each choral selection to help students learn basic musical skills, to discover to the cultural context in which the music was created, and to evaluate their own progress.

The Teacher Editions contain the same information as the student text, plus much additional background information, as well as suggested lesson plans, vocal warm-ups, and performance tips.

The repertoire books are designed to be used in conjunction with *Essential Musicianship*, Book 2, a comprehensive choral method for teaching vocal technique, sight-singing, and music theory.

How to Use *Essential Repertoire for the Developing Choir*

Each song is treated as an independent unit of study. Prior to each song is a page of information designed to be read by the student. Student pages consist of:

- Title and Composer, text information, and voicing/instrumentation.
- Cultural context of the song: Usually students can read and understand this section with limited guidance from the teacher.
- Musical terms: Students should be encouraged to find the listed terms in the song, and look up any unknown terms and/or symbols in the glossary.
- Preparation: Students will usually need teacher assistance in completing the Preparation section. This book is not designed to be student self-paced. Additional teaching suggestions, background information, and performance tips are included in the Teacher Edition.
- Evaluation: In most cases the Evaluation section is to be completed after the notes and rhythms of the piece have been mastered. Details for guiding the students' evaluation appear in the Teacher Edition.

Students should be encouraged to read the Cultural Context and Musical Terms sections of the text page prior to learning the song. This could be an effective activity for students while the teacher is involved in taking roll or other tasks. Students will usually need assistance in completing the rest of the text page.

The Teacher Edition

The Teacher Edition includes an extensive lesson plan for each choral selection which may be taught as suggested, expanded over a six-week period, or modified as needed. Each teaching plan contains the following:

- Student Text Page (slightly reduced in size)
- Ranges and song information (key, meter, form, performance possibilities)
- Learning objectives (Essential Elements) for each song correlated with the National Standards for Arts Education
- Historical/stylistic guidelines
- Answers to any student page questions
- Vocal technique/warm-ups/exercises
- Rehearsal guidelines and notes: 1) Suggested teaching sequence, and 2) Performance tips
- Evaluation suggestions for assessing student progress on the stated objectives
- Extension ideas

Who Should Use This Book

The authors of this text, all currently-practicing choral educators, bring a combined total of more than fifty years experience to the writing of this text. Their careful suggestions of tried and proven techniques provide a valuable resource of choral ideas for polishing performances.

Choral directors who are just entering the profession are encouraged to follow the suggested teaching sequence as written for each song to gain practical teaching skills.

Experienced choral directors may want to refer to the performance tips as a source of ideas for approaching a piece and refining it.

The warmups, vocalises, or polishing exercises included for every song in the Teacher Edition are particularly applicable to a given song. They also contain a wealth of ideas and suggestions which may be applied to other choral situations.

In Conclusion

Essential Repertoire for the Developing Choir, when combined with the companion volume *Essential Musicianship*, is in essence, a complete curriculum for the choral experience — a core library of repertoire aimed at awakening the singer's potential for self development, musical expression, and personal esteem.

ABOUT THE AUTHORS

JANICE KILLIAN received degrees from the University of Kansas, University of Connecticut, and earned her Ph.D. from the University of Texas-Austin. Throughout her career she has focused primarily on the junior high choral experience, but her teaching background includes public school experiences K-12 in Kansas, Connecticut, Minnesota, and Texas, as well as higher education experience at the State University of New York at Buffalo. Currently Dr. Killian is a member of the music education faculty at Texas Woman's University in Denton, Texas, where her duties include directing a choral ensemble, teaching graduate and undergraduate music education classes, and conducting music education research. She is the 1995 recipient of the prestigious Mary Mason Lyons Award for Distinguished Junior Faculty, granted for excellence in teaching, research, and service at Texas Woman's University.

MICHAEL O'HERN has been the choral director at Lake Highlands Junior High in Richardson, Texas, since the fall of 1982. A graduate of West Texas State University, Mr. O'Hern has completed graduate work at East Texas State University and The University of Texas at Arlington. A former Teacher of the Year in Richardson, Mr. O'Hearn is known nationally as a clinician and adjudicator and his choirs are consistent award-winners at local, state, and national competitions. Mr. O'Hearn is currently serving as Junior High/Middle School Vice President of the Texas Choral Directors Association. The Lake Highlands Junior High Chorale performed for the Texas Music Educators Convention in 1989 and 1994.

LINDA RANN has earned undergraduate and graduate degrees in Music Education from Louisiana State University in Baton Rouge with additional studies at Sam Houston State University, Texas Woman's University, University of North Texas, and Westminster Choir College. She is currently choral director at Dan Long Middle School in the Carrollton-Farmers Branch I.S.D., Carrollton, Texas, where her choirs are consistent sweepstakes winners. With over twenty years of public school teaching experience in elementary and middle school vocal music, Mrs. Rann is a frequent choral clinician and adjudicator. She has presented workshops nationally in the areas of middle school choral music and assessment in the performing arts.

ESSENTIAL ELEMENTS FOR CHOIR

The Method...

ESSENTIAL MUSICIANSHIP
A Comprehensive Choral Method
By Emily Crocker and John Leavitt

- Vocal technique
- Music theory skills
- Sight-reading skills
- Songs which encourage music reading
- Practical easy-to-use format
- One book works with all types of choirs – mixed, treble, tenor bass

Essential Musicianship - Book 1
(Recommended for Gr. 7-8)

08740069	Student
08740103	Teacher

Essential Musicianship - Book 2
(Recommended for Gr. 9-10)

08740104	Student
08740105	Teacher

Essential Musicianship - Book 3
(Recommended for Gr. 11-12)

08740106	Student
08740107	Teacher

For more information about *ESSENTIAL ELEMENTS FOR CHOIR*, contact your favorite choral retailer or write to:

ESSENTIAL ELEMENTS FOR CHOIR
Hal Leonard Corporation
7777 W. Bluemound Rd.
P.O. Box 13819
Milwaukee, WI 53213

ESSENTIAL ELEMENTS FOR CHOIR

A Complete Choral Experience for Grades 7-12

Created by educators for educators...a textbook to help (
singers achieve their full musical potential...and keep the
choir!

A two-faceted approach

The Repertoire...

ESSENTIAL REPERTOIRE
Choral Literature for Mixed, Treble,
and Tenor Bass Ensembles
By Glenda Casey, Bobbie Douglass, Jan Juneau, Janice
Killian, Michael O' Hern, Linda Rann and Brad White.
Edited by Emily Crocker.

- High quality, time-tested literature
- Objectives based on the National Standards for Arts Education
- Historical, stylistic guidelines and cultural context
- Choral techniques (including warm-ups, exercises, and drills)
- Rehearsal and performance tips
- Assessment techniques and enrichment ideas

Essential Repertoire for the Young Choir
(Recommended for Gr. 7-8)

08740070	Mixed/Student
08740108	Mixed/Teacher
08740071	Treble/Student
08740109	Treble/Teacher
08740096	Tenor Bass/Student
08740110	Tenor Bass/Teacher

Essential Repertoire for the
Developing Choir
(Recommended for Gr. 9-10)

08740111	Mixed/Student
08740113	Mixed/Teacher
08740095	Treble/Student
08740112	Treble/Teacher
08740115	Tenor Bass/Student
08740114	Tenor Bass/Teacher

Essential Repertoire for the Concert Choir
(Recommended for Gr. 10-11)

08740116	Mixed/Student
08740117	Mixed/Teacher
08740118	Treble/Student
08740120	Treble/Teacher
08740119	Tenor Bass/Student
08740121	Tenor Bass/Teacher

Essential Repertoire for the Concert
Choir-Artist Level
(Recommended for Gr. 11-12-Adult)

08740122	Mixed/Student
08740123	Mixed/Teacher
08740124	Treble/Student
08740126	Treble/Teacher
08740125	Tenor Bass/Student
08740127	Tenor Bass/Teacher